HSP Science

Lab Manual

Grade 3

Harcourt
SCHOOL PUBLISHERS

Visit *The Learning Site!*
www.harcourtschool.com

Copyright © by Harcourt, Inc.

All rights reserved. No part of this publication may be reproduced or transmitted in any form or by any means, electronic or mechanical, including photocopy, recording, or any information storage and retrieval system, without permission in writing from the publisher.

Permission is hereby granted to individuals using the corresponding student's textbook or kit as the major vehicle for regular classroom instruction to photocopy Copying Masters from this publication in classroom quantities for instructional use and not for resale. Requests for information on other matters regarding duplication of this work should be addressed to School Permissions and Copyrights, Harcourt, Inc., 6277 Sea Harbor Drive, Orlando, Florida 32887-6777. Fax: 407-345-2418.

HARCOURT and the Harcourt Logo are trademarks of Harcourt, Inc., registered in the United States of America and/or other jurisdictions.

Printed in the United States of America

ISBN-13: 978-0-15-361001-1
ISBN-10: 0-15-361001-8

2 3 4 5 6 7 8 9 10   073   16 15 14 13 12 11 10 09 08

If you have received these materials as examination copies free of charge, Harcourt School Publishers retains title to the materials and they may not be resold. Resale of examination copies is strictly prohibited and is illegal.

Possession of this publication in print format does not entitle users to convert this publication, or any portion of it, into electronic format.

Contents

Safety in Science LM1
Science Safety Checklist LM2
Using Science Tools LM3

Unit Inquiry Log LM9

Getting Ready for Science

Lesson 1 Investigate Log LM13
            Independent Inquiry LM15
Lesson 2 Investigate Log LM16
            Independent Inquiry LM18
Lesson 3 Investigate Log LM19
            Independent Inquiry LM21

Unit A Unit Inquiry Log LM22

Chapter 1: Types of Living Things

Lesson 1 Investigate Log LM26
            Independent Inquiry LM28
Lesson 2 Investigate Log LM29
            Independent Inquiry LM31

Chapter 2: Types of Plants

Lesson 1 Investigate Log LM32
Independent Inquiry LM34
Lesson 2 Investigate Log LM35
Independent Inquiry LM37
Lesson 3 Investigate Log LM38
Independent Inquiry LM40

Chapter 3: Types of Animals

Lesson 1 Investigate Log LM41
Independent Inquiry LM43
Lesson 2 Investigate Log LM44
Independent Inquiry LM46
Lesson 3 Investigate Log LM47
Independent Inquiry LM49

Unit B Unit Inquiry Log....................... LM50

Chapter 4: Where Living Things Are Found

Lesson 1 Investigate Log LM54
Independent Inquiry LM56
Lesson 2 Investigate Log LM57
Independent Inquiry LM59
Lesson 3 Investigate Log LM60
Independent Inquiry LM62
Lesson 4 Investigate Log LM63
Independent Inquiry LM65

Chapter 5: Living Things Depend on One Another

Lesson 1 Investigate Log LM66
Independent Inquiry LM68
Lesson 2 Investigate Log LM69
Independent Inquiry LM71
Lesson 3 Investigate Log LM72
Independent Inquiry LM74

Unit C Unit Inquiry Log........................ LM75

Chapter 6: Minerals and Rocks

Lesson 1 Investigate Log LM79
Independent Inquiry LM81
Lesson 2 Investigate Log LM82
Independent Inquiry LM84
Lesson 3 Investigate Log LM85
Independent Inquiry LM87

Chapter 7: Forces that Shape the Land

Lesson 1 Investigate Log LM88
Independent Inquiry LM90
Lesson 2 Investigate Log LM91
Independent Inquiry LM93
Lesson 3 Investigate Log LM94
Independent Inquiry LM96

Chapter 8: Conserving Resources

Lesson 1 Investigate Log	LM97
Independent Inquiry	LM99
Lesson 2 Investigate Log	LM100
Independent Inquiry	LM102
Lesson 3 Investigate Log	LM103
Independent Inquiry	LM105
Lesson 4 Investigate Log	LM106
Independent Inquiry	LM108
Unit D Unit Inquiry Log	**LM109**

Chapter 9: The Water Cycle

Lesson 1 Investigate Log	LM113
Independent Inquiry	LM115
Lesson 2 Investigate Log	LM116
Independent Inquiry	LM118
Lesson 3 Investigate Log	LM119
Independent Inquiry	LM121

Chapter 10: Earth's Place in the Solar System

Lesson 1 Investigate Log	LM122
Independent Inquiry	LM124
Lesson 2 Investigate Log	LM125
Independent Inquiry	LM127
Lesson 3 Investigate Log	LM128
Independent Inquiry	LM130
Unit E Unit Inquiry Log	**LM131**

Chapter 11 Properties of Matter

Lesson 1 Investigate Log LM135
          Independent Inquiry LM137
Lesson 2 Investigate Log LM138
          Independent Inquiry LM140
Lesson 3 Investigate Log LM141
          Independent Inquiry LM143

Chapter 12 Energy

Lesson 1 Investigate Log LM144
          Independent Inquiry LM146
Lesson 2 Investigate Log LM147
          Independent Inquiry LM149
Lesson 3 Investigate Log LM150
          Independent Inquiry LM152

Chapter 13 Electricity and Magnets

Lesson 1 Investigate Log LM153
          Independent Inquiry LM155
Lesson 2 Investigate Log LM156
          Independent Inquiry LM158
Lesson 3 Investigate Log LM159
          Independent Inquiry LM161

Chapter 14 Heat, Light, and Sound

Lesson 1 Investigate Log LM162
            Independent Inquiry LM164
Lesson 2 Investigate Log LM165
            Independent Inquiry LM167
Lesson 3 Investigate Log LM168
            Independent Inquiry LM170
Lesson 4 Investigate Log LM171
            Independent Inquiry LM173

Unit F Unit Inquiry Log....................... LM174

Chapter 15 Forces and Motion

Lesson 1 Investigate Log LM178
            Independent Inquiry LM180
Lesson 2 Investigate Log LM181
            Independent Inquiry LM183
Lesson 3 Investigate Log LM184
            Independent Inquiry LM186

Chapter 16 Work and Machines

Lesson 1 Investigate Log LM187
            Independent Inquiry LM189
Lesson 2 Investigate Log LM190
            Independent Inquiry LM192
Lesson 3 Investigate Log LM193
            Independent Inquiry LM195

Science Fair Project Ideas LM196

Safety in Science

Doing investigations in science can be fun, but you need to be sure you do them safely. Here are some rules to follow.

1. **Think ahead.** Study the steps of the investigation so you know what to expect. If you have any questions, ask your teacher. Be sure you understand any caution statements or safety reminders.

2. **Be neat.** Keep your work area clean. If you have long hair, pull it back so it doesn't get in the way. Roll or push up long sleeves to keep them away from your experiment.

3. **Oops!** If you spill or break something, or if you get cut, tell your teacher right away.

4. **Watch your eyes.** Wear safety goggles anytime you are directed to do so. If you get anything in your eyes, tell your teacher right away.

5. **Yuck!** Never eat or drink anything during a science activity.

6. **Don't get shocked.** Be especially careful if an electric appliance is used. Be sure that electric cords are in a safe place where you can't trip over them. Never pull a plug out of an outlet by pulling on the cord.

7. **Keep it clean.** Always clean up when you have finished. Put everything away and wipe your work area. Wash your hands.

8. **Play it safe.** Always know where safety equipment, such as fire extinguishers, can be found. Be familiar with how to use the safety equipment around you.

Name _____

Date _____

Science Safety

____ I will study the steps of the investigation before I begin.

____ I will ask my teacher if I do not understand something.

____ I will keep my work area clean.

____ I will pull my hair back and roll up long sleeves before I begin.

____ I will tell my teacher if I spill or break something or get cut.

____ I will wear safety goggles when I am told to do so.

____ I will tell my teacher if I get something in my eye.

____ I will not eat or drink anything during an investigation unless told to do so by my teacher.

____ I will be extra careful when using electrical appliances.

____ I will keep electric cords out of the way and only unplug them by pulling on the protected plug.

____ I will clean up when I am finished.

____ I will return unused materials to my teacher.

____ I will wipe my area and then wash my hands.

LM 2 Science Safety Checklist

Using Science Tools

In almost every science inquiry in this lab manual, you will use tools to observe, measure, and compare the things that you are studying. Each tool is used for a different thing. Part of learning about science is learning how to choose tools to help you answer questions. Here are some tools that you might use and some rules on how to use them.

Using a Hand Lens

Use a hand lens to magnify an object. *Magnify* means "to make something look larger."

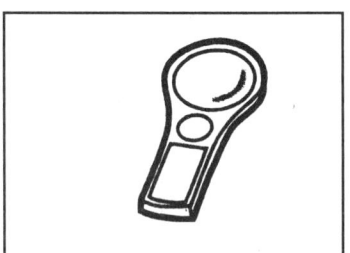

1. Hold a hand lens about 12 centimeters (5 inches) from your eye.
2. Bring the object toward you until it comes into focus, which means it is not blurry.

Using a Magnifying Box

Use a magnifying box to magnify something on a flat surface. You can put things inside the box to observe. The magnifying box can be used to observe small living things such as insects. You can observe the insect and then release it.

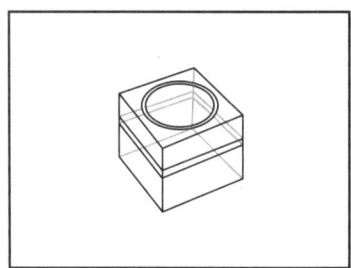

1. Place the magnifying box on top of a flat surface.
2. Place the object you want to observe inside the box. Put on the lid.
3. Look through the lid at the insect or object.

Safety: Do not use a hand lens or magnifying box that is cracked or damaged. If one breaks, do not try to clean up the broken pieces. Call your teacher for help.

Using a Thermometer

Use a thermometer to measure temperature.
Temperature means "how hot or cold something is."

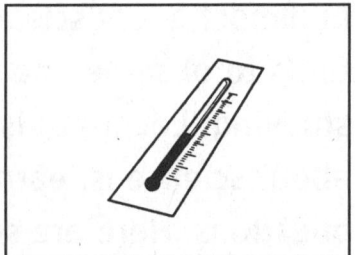

1. Place the thermometer in the liquid. Never stir the liquid with the thermometer. Don't touch the thermometer any more than you need to. When you are measuring the temperature of the air, stand between the thermometer and bright lights, such as sunlight.

2. When you are measuring something that is not being heated or cooled, wait about five minutes for the temperature reading to stop changing. When the thing you are measuring is being heated or cooled, you will not be able to wait. Read the temperature quickly.

3. To read the temperature, move so that your eyes are even with the liquid in the thermometer. Find the scale line that meets the top of the liquid in the thermometer, and read the temperature.

Safety: If a thermometer breaks, call your teacher for help.

Using Forceps

Use forceps to pick up and hold on to objects.

1. To pick up an object, place the tips of the forceps around the object. Press the forceps' handles together with your thumb and first finger to grab the object.

2. Move the object to where you want to place it. Stop pressing with your thumb and first finger. The forceps will let go of the object.

Safety: The tips of forceps can be sharp. Keep forceps away from your face.

Using a Ruler or Meterstick

Use a ruler or a meterstick to measure dimensions of objects and distances. *Dimensions* **are the sizes of things, such as** *length, width, height,* **and** *depth.*

1. Place the zero mark or end of the ruler next to the left end of the object you want to measure.
2. On the other end of the ruler, find the place next to the right end of the object.
3. Look at the scale on the ruler next to the right end of the object. This will show you the length of the object.
4. A meterstick works the same way. You can use it to measure longer objects.
5. You also can use a ruler or meterstick to measure the distance between two places.

Safety: Some rulers and metersticks can have sharp edges. Be careful not to cut yourself. Never point a ruler or meterstick at another person.

Using a Tape Measure

Use a tape measure to measure around curved objects or to measure distances longer than a ruler or meterstick.

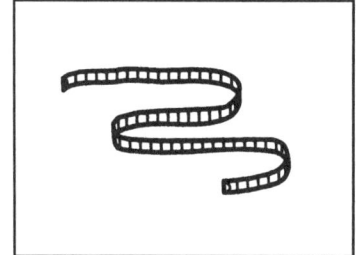

1. Place the tape measure around the object or along the distance you would like to measure.
2. Read the tape measure the same way you would read a ruler or meterstick.
3. When you are measuring long distances with a tape measure, you will need a lab partner to hold one end while you stretch the tape measure to the other end of the distance.

Using Science Tools | **LM 5**

Using a Balance

Use a balance to measure mass. *Mass* means "how much matter something has."

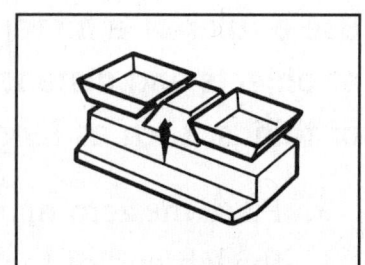

1. Look at the pointer on the base to see that it points at the middle mark of its scale.

2. Place the object that you wish to measure in the pan on the left side of the balance. The pointer should move away from the middle scale mark.

3. Add standard masses to the pan on the right side of the balance. As you add masses, you should see the pointer move back toward the middle scale mark. When the pointer stays at the middle mark, the mass is the same in both pans.

4. Add the numbers on the standard masses that you placed in the pan on the right side of the balance. The total is the mass of the object you measured.

Using a Spring Scale

Use a spring scale to measure an object's weight or a force. *Force* means "how hard you lift or pull on something."

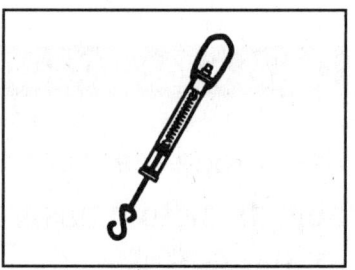

Measuring Weight

1. Hook the spring scale to the object.

2. Lift the scale and object with a smooth motion. Do not jerk the object upward.

3. Wait until the spring stops moving. Then read the force on the scale.

4. You can measure objects that will not fit on the hook. Put the object in a light plastic bag. Hang the bag on the hook.

Using a Measuring Cup, a Beaker, or a Graduated Cylinder

Use a measuring cup to measure the volume of a liquid or a loose solid such as powder. *Volume* **means "how much space something fills."**

Measuring Liquids

1. Pour the liquid you want to measure into a measuring cup. Put your measuring cup on a flat surface, with the measuring scale facing you.

2. Look at the liquid through the cup. Move so that your eyes are even with the surface of the liquid in the cup. To read the volume of the liquid, find the scale line that is even with the surface of the liquid.

3. When the surface of the liquid is not exactly even with a line, decide which line the liquid is closer to and use that number.

4. Beakers and graduated cylinders are used in the same way as measuring cups. They can have different shapes and sizes.

Measuring Solids

- You can measure a solid, such as sand or powder, in the same way that you measure a liquid. You will have to smooth out the top of the solid before you can read the volume.

Safety: Some measuring cups, beakers, and graduated cylinders are made of glass. Be careful not to drop one or it could break.

Using a Dropper

Use a dropper to move tiny amounts of liquid.

1. Hold the dropper upright. Put the tip of the dropper in the liquid.

2. Gently squeeze the bulb on the dropper. Stop squeezing to allow the liquid to fill the dropper.

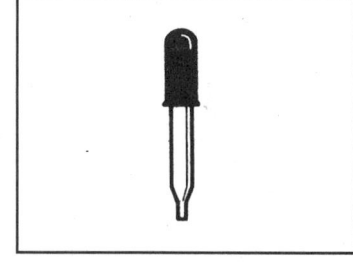

Using Science Tools　LM 7

3. Hold the dropper over the place where you want to put the liquid. Gently squeeze the bulb to release one drop at a time.

Safety: Never put a dropper in your mouth. Do not use a dropper that you use in science class for medicine, especially eye drops.

Using a Microscope

Use a microscope to magnify very small objects. A microscope is much more powerful than a simple hand lens.

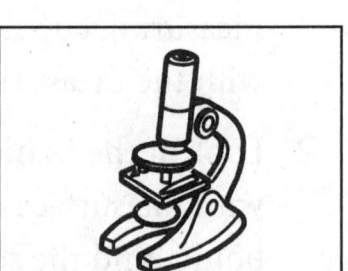

Caring for a Microscope

- Carry a microscope with two hands, use a rolling cart to move it, or ask a teacher for help.
- Never touch any of the lenses of a microscope with your fingers.

Using a Standard Microscope

1. Raise the eyepiece as far as you can by turning the coarse-adjustment knob. Place your slide on the stage.

2. Turn the lowest-power lens into place. The lowest-power lens is usually the shortest. Slowly use the adjustment knobs to lower the eyepiece and lens to the lowest position it can go without touching the slide.

3. Look through the eyepiece, and raise the eyepiece and lens with the coarse-adjustment knob until the object on the slide is almost in focus. Then use the fine-adjustment knob to focus.

4. When you need to magnify the object on the slide even more, turn the higher-power lens into place. Make sure that the lens does not touch the slide. Use only the fine-adjustment knob to move the eyepiece and lens when looking through a higher-power lens.

Name _____

Date _____

Inquiry Log

Use these pages to plan and conduct a science experiment to answer a question you may have.

1. Observe and Ask Questions

Make a list of questions you have about a topic. Then circle a question you want to investigate.

_____

2. Form a Hypothesis

Write a hypothesis. A hypothesis is a scientific explanation that you can test.

_____

3. Plan an Experiment

Identify and Control Variables

To plan your experiment, you must first identify the important variables. Complete the statements below.

The variable I will change is

_____.

The variables I will observe or measure are

_____.

The variables I will keep the same, or *control*, are

_____.

(page 1 of 4)　　　　Lab Manual　LM 9

Name _____

Develop a Procedure and Gather Materials Write the steps you will follow to set up an experiment and collect data.

_____
_____
_____
_____
_____
_____
_____

Use extra sheets of blank paper if you need to write down more steps.

Materials List Look carefully at all the steps of your procedure, and list all the materials you will use. Be sure that your teacher approves your plan and your materials list before you begin.

_____
_____
_____
_____
_____
_____

Name _____

Inquiry Log

4. Conduct the Experiment

Gather and Record Data Follow your plan and collect data. Make a table to record your data. **Observe** carefully. **Record** your observations and be sure to note anything unusual or unexpected. Use the space below and additional paper if necessary.

_____
_____
_____
_____
_____
_____
_____
_____
_____
_____
_____
_____
_____

Name _____

Inquiry Log

Interpret Data Make a graph of the data you have collected. Plot the data on a sheet of graph paper or use a software program.

5. **Draw Conclusions and Communicate Results**

   Compare the hypothesis with the data and the graph. Then answer these questions.

   1. Given the results of the experiment, do you think the hypothesis is true? Explain.

   _____

   _____

   2. How would you revise the hypothesis? Explain.

   _____

   _____

   3. What else did you **observe** during the experiment?

   _____

   _____

Prepare a presentation for your classmates to **communicate** what you have learned. Display your data tables and graphs.

Investigate Further

Write another hypothesis that you might investigate.

_____

_____

LM 12 Lab Manual   (page 4 of 4)

Name _____

Date _____

Making Bubbles

Materials

metric measuring cup    water    large container 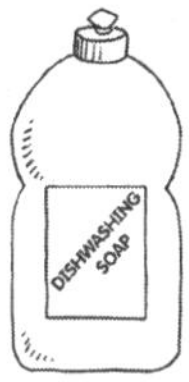   dishwashing soap

safety goggles   stirring stick    straw 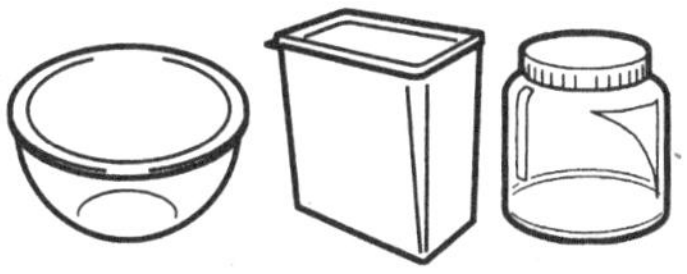   small containers    hand lens

Procedure

1. **CAUTION:** Put on safety goggles. Use the metric measuring cup to **measure** 1 L (1,000 mL) of water. Pour the water into a large container.

2. Use the measuring cup to **measure** 50 mL of dishwashing soap. Add the dishwashing soap to the container of water. Stir the soap and water together.

3. Pour some of the soap-and-water solution into small containers. Use the straw to blow air into the solution. Be careful not to blow too hard or to spill some of the solution. Bubbles should form. **Observe** the bubbles with a hand lens. **Record** your **observations**.

Draw what you see when you look at the bubbles with a hand lens.

Use with pages 4–5.

Name _____

Investigate Log

Draw Conclusions

1. What did you **observe** about the bubbles?

   _____
   _____
   _____

2. **Inquiry Skill—*Measure*** Scientists use many different tools to **measure** things. In this Investigate, you used a measuring cup to **measure** both water and soap. What kind of measuring tool could you use to **measure** the size of the bubbles you made? Explain your answer.

   _____
   _____
   _____

Inquiry Skill Tip

A **measurement** includes a number and a unit. Suppose the width of a bubble is 6 centimeters. This measurement includes the number 6 and the unit centimeters. Other units are ounces, pounds, inches, miles, seconds, and liters.

Investigate Self-Assessment	Agree	Not Sure	Disagree
I made bubbles by blowing into soap and water.			
I was careful not to get any of the soap and water into my mouth.			
I **measured** the water and the dishwashing soap.			

LM 14   Lab Manual   (page 2 of 3)   Use with pages 4–5.

Name _____
Date _____

Independent Inquiry

Add 60 mL of glycerine and 8 mL of sugar to the solution. Blow bubbles. Compare these bubbles to the first bubbles.

Materials

Here are some materials that you might use.
List additional materials that you need.

- metric measuring cup
- hand lens
- straw
- water
- small containers
- stirring stick
- glycerine
- sugar
- dishwashing soap
- large container
- safety goggles

1. Predict how the bubbles made with glycerine and sugar will be different from the first bubbles that you made.

   _____

   _____

2. In the space below, draw what you see when you look at the bubbles with a hand lens.

3. Compare the glycerine and sugar bubbles to the regular bubbles. How are they alike and different?

   _____

   _____

   _____

Use with page 5.   (page 3 of 3)   Lab Manual   LM 15

Name _____

Date _____

Investigate Log

Shapes of Bubbles

Materials

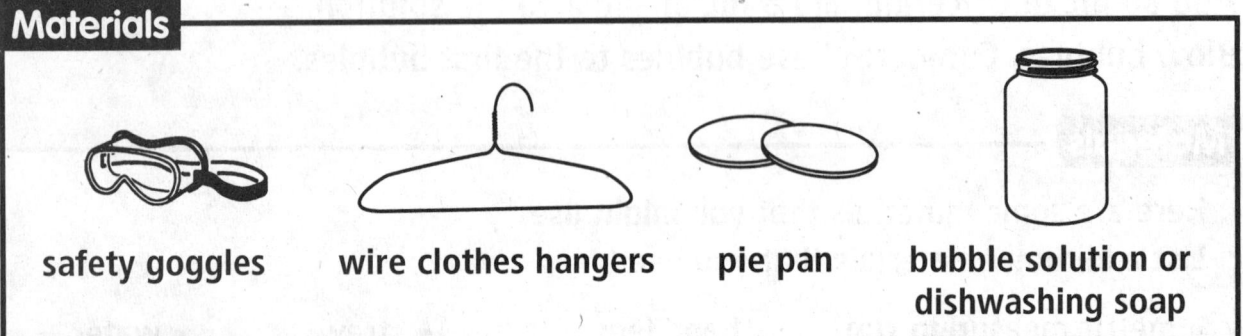

safety goggles | wire clothes hangers | pie pan | bubble solution or dishwashing soap

Procedure

① **CAUTION: Put on safety goggles.** Use wire hangers to make bubble wands of different shapes. For example, you could make a round, a square, and a triangular wand.

② **Predict** the shape of the bubbles that will be made by each wand.

③ Pour some of the bubble solution into the pie pan. Dip one of your wands into the solution. Use the wand to make bubbles. **Observe** the shapes of the bubbles. Repeat this activity with all of the wands that you made.

Wand	Sketch of Wand Shape	Bubble Shape	Other Observations
1			
2			
3			

LM 16   Lab Manual   (page 1 of 3)   Use with pages 16–17.

Name _____

Investigate Log

Draw Conclusions

1. What did you **predict** about the shape of the bubbles? Were your **predictions** correct?

   _____
   _____
   _____
   _____

2. **Inquiry Skill—*Predict*** Scientists use **observations** of the natural world to make **predictions**. Use your **observations** to **predict** the shape of a bubble blown with a heart-shaped wand.

   _____
   _____
   _____

Inquiry Skill Tip

Good **predictions** are not random guesses. They are educated guesses based on past experience. Before you make a prediction, review any observations, data, or experiments that suggest what might happen in the future.

Investigate Self-Assessment	Agree	Not Sure	Disagree
I made bubble wands in different shapes.			
I obeyed safety rules and was careful when using wire hangers to make bubble wands.			
I **predicted** the shape of the bubbles made with each wand.			

Use with pages 16–17.   (page 2 of 3)   Lab Manual **LM 17**

Name _____
Date _____

Independent Inquiry

What wand shape would make the biggest bubble? Blow bubbles with different wands. Measure and compare the bubbles' sizes.

Materials

Here are some materials that you might use.
List additional materials that you need.
- wire clothes hangers
- bubble solution
- safety goggles
- pie pan

1. Explain how you will measure or estimate the size of each bubble.

   _____

   _____

   _____

   _____

2. Blow bubbles with different wands. Make a table to record the results.

Wand	Sketch of Wand Shape	Estimated Size of Bubble
1		
2		
3		

3. Which wand shape made the biggest bubble?

   _____

   _____

LM 18 Lab Manual   (page 3 of 3)   Use with page 17.

Name _____
Date _____

Bubble Colors

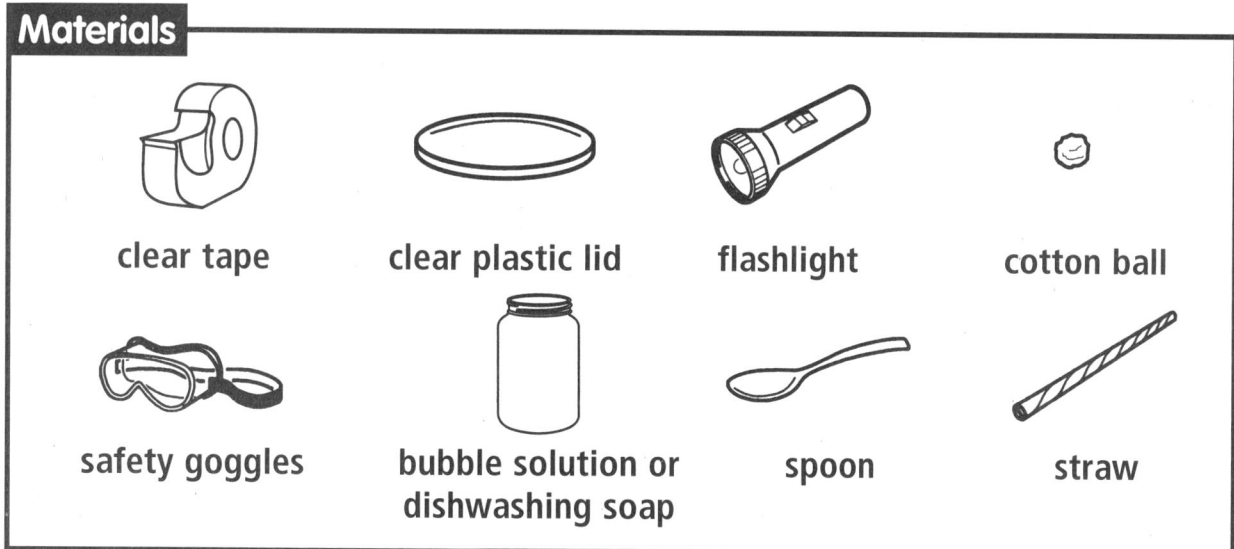

Materials: clear tape, clear plastic lid, flashlight, cotton ball, safety goggles, bubble solution or dishwashing soap, spoon, straw

Procedure

1 **CAUTION:** Put on safety goggles. Tape the plastic lid over the part of the flashlight that light shines from.

2 Hold the flashlight so the light will shine straight up. Dip a cotton ball in the bubble solution. Wipe the cotton ball over the top of the lid. Make sure you wet the whole lid. Then put a spoonful of the solution on the lid.

3 Use a straw to blow one big bubble. Turn off the lights, and hold the flashlight so that the attached lid is about even with your eyebrows.

4 **Observe** the bubble. Dip the end of the straw in bubble solution, and put the straw inside the big bubble. Blow very gently. **Observe** what happens.

Observations before blowing:
Observations while blowing:
Observations during popping:

Use with pages 28–29.   (page 1 of 3)   Lab Manual **LM 19**

Name _____

Investigate Log

Draw Conclusions

1. **Communicate** your **observations** by drawing what happened.

   [ ]

2. **Inquiry Skill—*Compare*** Use your **observations** to **compare** the colors in the bubble when you first watched it to the colors you saw right before the bubble popped.

   _____
   _____
   _____

> **Inquiry Skill Tip**
>
> **Compare** means to tell how things are alike and different. When you compare, tell at least one way things are alike and at least one way they are different.

Investigate Self-Assessment	Agree	Not Sure	Disagree
I followed the directions for observing bubble colors.			
I was careful not to get the bubble solution into my mouth.			
I **compared** the colors in the bubble at different times.			

LM 20 Lab Manual   (page 2 of 3)   Use with pages 28–29.

Name _____
Date _____

Independent Inquiry

Predict how adding some tempera paint to bubbles will change the Investigate. Plan and conduct a simple experiment to test your predictions.

Materials

Here are some materials that you might use.
List additional materials that you need.

- clear tape
- clear plastic lid
- flashlight
- cotton ball
- bubble solution
- spoon
- straw
- tempera paint
- safety goggles

1. Predict how the paint will change your observations of the bubble.

   _____
   _____

2. Conduct your experiment. Record your observations.

   _____
   _____
   _____

3. Did the results support your prediction? Explain.

   _____
   _____

Use with page 29. Lab Manual **LM 21**

Name _____
Date _____

Unit A

Body Coverings

1. **Observe and Ask Questions**

   Animals have many adaptations to help them survive in their environments. Mammals are the only animals that have hair. What does hair do for a mammal? Make a list of questions you have about hair. Then circle a question you want to investigate.

   _____

2. **Form a Hypothesis**

   Write a hypothesis. A hypothesis is a suggested answer to the question you are investigating. You must be able to test the hypothesis.

   _____

3. **Plan an Experiment**

   Identify and Control Variables

   To plan your experiment, you must first identify the important variables. Complete the statements below.

   The variable I will change is

   _____.

   The variables I will observe or measure are

   _____.

   The variables I will keep the same, or *control*, are

   _____.

LM 22   Lab Manual   (page 1 of 4)   Use with page 47.

Name _____

Unit Inquiry Log

Develop a Procedure and Gather Materials Write the steps you will follow to set up an experiment and collect data.

_____
_____
_____
_____
_____
_____
_____
_____

Use extra sheets of blank paper if you need to write down more steps.

Materials List Look carefully at all the steps of your procedure, and list all the materials you will use. Be sure that your teacher approves your plan and your materials list before you begin.

_____
_____
_____
_____

Name _____

4. Conduct the Experiment

Gather and Record Data Follow your plan and collect data. Use the chart below or a chart you design to record your data. **Observe** carefully. **Record** your observations and be sure to note anything unusual or unexpected.

Amount of Time in Refrigerator _____

Room Temperature _____

Amount of Hair on Animal	Temperature After Being in Cold

LM 24 Lab Manual   (page 3 of 4)   Use with page 47.

Name _____

Unit Inquiry Log

Interpret Data Make graphs of the data you have collected. Plot the data on a sheet of graph paper or use a software program.

5. **Draw Conclusions and Communicate Results**

   Compare the **hypothesis** with the data and the graphs. Then answer these questions.

   1. Given the results of the experiment, do you think the hypothesis was correct? Explain.

   _____
   _____

   2. How would you revise the hypothesis? Explain.

   _____
   _____

   3. What else did you **observe** during the experiment?

   _____
   _____

Prepare a presentation for your classmates to **communicate** what you have learned. Display your data tables and graphs.

Investigate Further

Write another hypothesis that you might investigate.

_____
_____

Use with page 47.   (page 4 of 4)   Lab Manual   LM 25

Name _____
Date _____

Homes for Living Things

Materials

picture sorting cards   crayons or colored pencils   paper

Procedure

1 Look at the picture sorting cards your teacher has given you. Sort the cards into two piles—one for living things and one for things that are not living.

2 Choose an animal from the stack of cards that show living things.

3 Describe what makes the animal a living thing. Then describe where the animal lives. **Record** your **observations**.

4 Suppose you work at a zoo. Use crayons or colored pencils to draw a habitat for your animal. Draw everything your animal might need.

5 **Compare** the home for your animal with the homes your classmates drew.

What makes the animal a living thing?	Where does the animal live?

LM 26   Lab Manual   (page 1 of 3)   Use with pages 52–53.

Name _____

Investigate Log

Draw Conclusions

1. What did you **observe** about the home where your animal lives?

   _____

   _____

   _____

2. **Inquiry Skill—*Infer*** Infer what an animal gets from its home. Why does that animal live where it does?

   _____

   _____

   _____

Inquiry Skill Tip

When you make an **inference**, you are making a logical statement about what you have observed. You can test your inference by using it to finish the sentence, "It makes sense that...."

Investigate Self-Assessment	Agree	Not Sure	Disagree
I observed the picture cards and drew a habitat according to the directions for this investigation.			
I put away the materials for this activity when I was finished.			
I made an **inference** about animals and their homes.			

Use with pages 52–53.   (page 2 of 3)   Lab Manual   LM 27

Name _____
Date _____

Investigate Log

Independent Inquiry

Look at the cards. Compare the body coverings of several animals. Classify the animals by the types of body coverings they have.

Materials

Here are some materials that you might use.
List additional materials that you need.

- picture sorting cards

1. What is the purpose of this investigation?

   _____

   _____

2. Use this space to show how you classify the animals.

Type of body covering	Animals with that type of body covering

3. Pick one of your groups of animals that all have the same type of body covering. How are these animals alike and different?

   _____

   _____

   _____

LM 28 Lab Manual   (page 3 of 3)   Use with page 53.

Name _____
Date _____

Investigate Log

How Fast Do Seeds Grow?

Materials

- paper towels
- 3 small zip-top bags
- water
- tape
- 3 kinds of seeds
- ruler

Procedure

1. Fold three paper towels to fit inside a plastic bag. Place one paper towel into each bag with a small amount of water. Be careful not to make the paper towels too wet.

2. Number the bags 1, 2, and 3. Put your name on each bag.

3. Place seeds of one kind in bag 1, another kind in bag 2, and the third kind in bag 3. Zip the bags and place them near a sunny window.

4. For five days, use a ruler to **measure** how much each seed has grown each day. **Record** your **observations** in the table below.

5. Add water to the bags if you notice the paper towels drying out.

Seeds	Day 1	Day 2	Day 3	Day 4	Day 5
Bag #1					
Bag #2					
Bag #3					

Use with pages 62–63.   (page 1 of 3)   Lab Manual   LM 29

Name _____

Investigate Log

Draw Conclusions

1. What changes did you **observe** in each bag?

   _____

   _____

   _____

2. **Inquiry Skill—*Infer*** Infer what will happen if you leave the seeds near the window longer than five days.

   _____

   _____

   _____

> **Inquiry Skill Tip**
>
> To make an **inference**, make a list of all your data. Then write a sentence to explain what your data shows.

Investigate Self-Assessment	Agree	Not Sure	Disagree
I prepared the bags according to the directions for this investigation.			
I used the ruler to measure the seeds' growth.			
I made an **inference** about how seeds grow.			

LM 30 Lab Manual   (page 2 of 3)   Use with pages 62–63.

Name _____

Date _____

Investigate Log

Independent Inquiry

Will seeds sprout without light? Predict what would happen if you placed new bags of seeds in a dark closet instead of in a sunny window. Try it.

Materials

Here are some materials that you might use.
List additional materials that you need.

- paper towels
- 3 small zip-top bags
- water
- tape
- 3 kinds of seeds
- ruler

1. What do you predict will happen with the seeds that are placed in the dark?

   _____

   _____

2. Use this table to record your observations.

Seeds	Day 1	Day 2	Day 3	Day 4	Day 5
Bag #1					
Bag #2					
Bag #3					

3. Did your prediction match your results? Explain.

   _____

   _____

   _____

Use with page 63.   (page 3 of 3)   Lab Manual   LM 31

Name _____
Date _____

Investigate Log

Needs of Plants

Materials

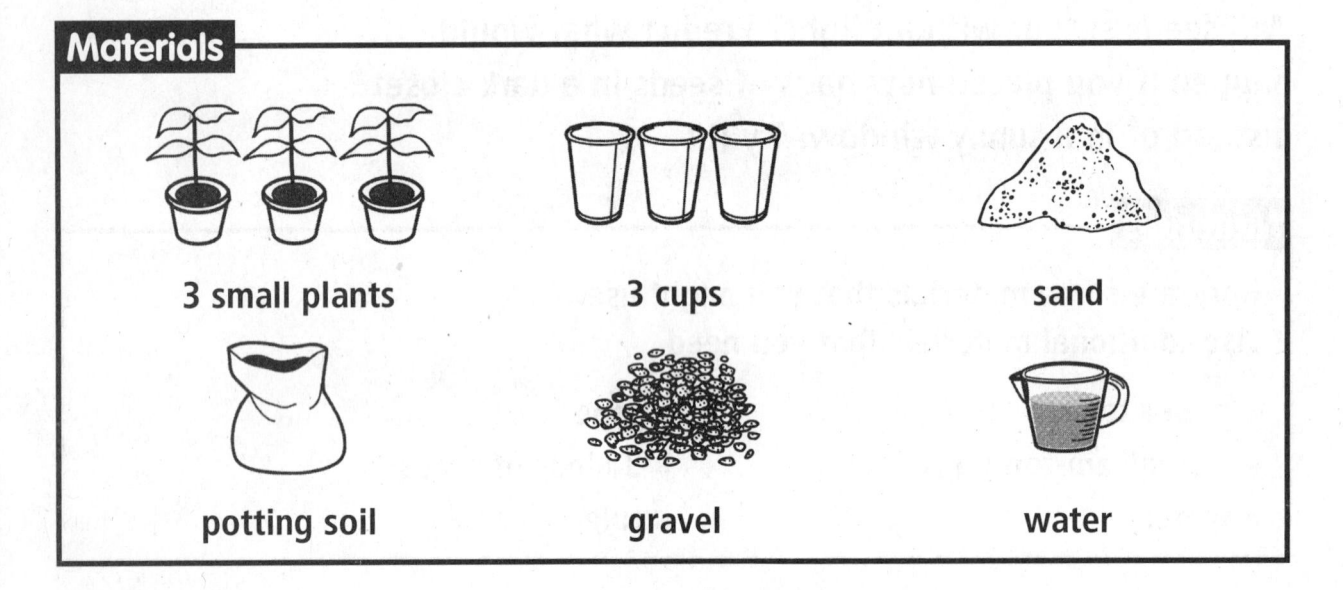

- 3 small plants
- 3 cups
- sand
- potting soil
- gravel
- water

Procedure

1. Take 3 plants. Gently shake the soil from each plant. Plant one in a cup of sand. Plant another in a cup of gravel. Plant the third in a cup of soil. Water each plant. Put the cups in a sunny window.

2. **Observe** the plants every other day for two weeks. Water the plants every few days with the same amount of water.

3. **Record** any changes you **observe**. Make sure to look for changes in plant size.

Day	Plant 1 (Sand)	Plant 2 (Gravel)	Plant 3 (Soil)
2			
4			
6			
8			
10			
12			
14			

LM 32 Lab Manual

Name _____

Investigate Log

Draw Conclusions

1. Which plant looked the healthiest after two weeks? Explain why.

   _____

   _____

   _____

Inquiry Skill Tip

You can make it easier to **compare** three objects by comparing them in pairs first. Compare 1 and 2, 1 and 3, and then 2 and 3.

2. Which plant looked the least healthy after two weeks? What was different for this plant?

   _____

   _____

3. **Inquiry Skill—*Compare*** Scientists often **compare** the results they get in their experiments. How could you compare your findings?

   _____

   _____

Investigate Self-Assessment	Agree	Not Sure	Disagree
I planted the three plants according to the directions for this investigation.			
I washed my hands after working with the plants and soil.			
I **compared** the plants by characteristics such as height, color, and number of leaves.			

Use with pages 78–79.　　　(page 2 of 3)　　　Lab Manual　LM 33

Name _____
Date _____

Investigate Log

Independent Inquiry

Predict how different amounts of water might affect the growth of plants. Try it!

Materials

Here are some materials that you might use.
List additional materials that you need.

- 3 small plants
- potting soil
- 3 cups
- water

1. Predict how the amount of water will affect the growth of plants.

   _____
   _____
   _____

2. Make a table to record the results of your investigation of how the amount of water affects plant growth.

3. Explain how the outcome of your investigation compares to your prediction.

   _____
   _____
   _____

LM 34 Lab Manual (page 3 of 3) Use with page 79.

Name _____
Date _____

Investigate Log

Growing Lima Beans

Materials

3 lima bean seeds | 2 zip-top plastic bags | hand lens | water | 2 paper towels

Procedure

1. Split one lima bean seed in half, and use the hand lens to look inside. Identify the new plant inside the seed. After you have finished, put the seed to the side.

2. Fold each paper towel in half. Moisten one of them with water, but don't use too much water. Don't moisten the other towel. Then place each towel inside a plastic bag.

3. Place one seed in each bag. Label the bag with the moistened towel *WET,* and label the other bag *DRY.* Seal the bags, and place them where they won't be disturbed.

4. Make a table. **Observe** the seeds for 10 school days. **Record** your **observations**.

Day	Wet Seed	Dry Seed
1		
2		
3		
4		
5		
6		
7		
8		
9		
10		

Use with pages 88–89.

Name _____

Investigate Log

Draw Conclusions

1. How does a new bean plant grow?

   _____

   _____

2. **Inquiry Skill**—*Draw Conclusions* Use what you have observed to **draw conclusions** about what bean seeds need to grow. Why do you think the seeds didn't need soil to start growing?

   _____

   _____

   _____

Inquiry Skill Tip

You **draw conclusions** from observations and facts. After an investigation, make a list of what you know, and then use the list to make and support a conclusion.

Investigate Self-Assessment	Agree	Not Sure	Disagree
I observed the inside of a lima bean.			
I washed my hands after handling the lima beans.			
I **drew a conclusion** from my observation of the inside of a lima bean and the lima beans in the paper towels.			

LM 36 Lab Manual   (page 2 of 3)   Use with pages 88–89.

Name _____

Date _____

Investigate Log

Independent Inquiry

Predict how seeds will grow at different temperatures. Design and conduct an experiment to see if seeds grow faster in warm or cold weather.

Materials

Here are some materials that you might use. List additional materials that you need.

- 2 lima bean seeds
- 2 zip-top plastic bags
- water
- 2 paper towels

1. Do you think the lima bean seeds will grow faster in warm or cold weather? Explain.

   _____

   _____

2. Use the table below to record your observations.

Day	Warm Environment	Cold Environment
1		
2		
3		
4		
5		
6		
7		

3. Did the results of your investigation agree or disagree with your prediction? Explain.

   _____

   _____

Use with page 89.   (page 3 of 3)   Lab Manual   LM 37

Name _____
Date _____

Investigate Log

Lights, Plants, Action!

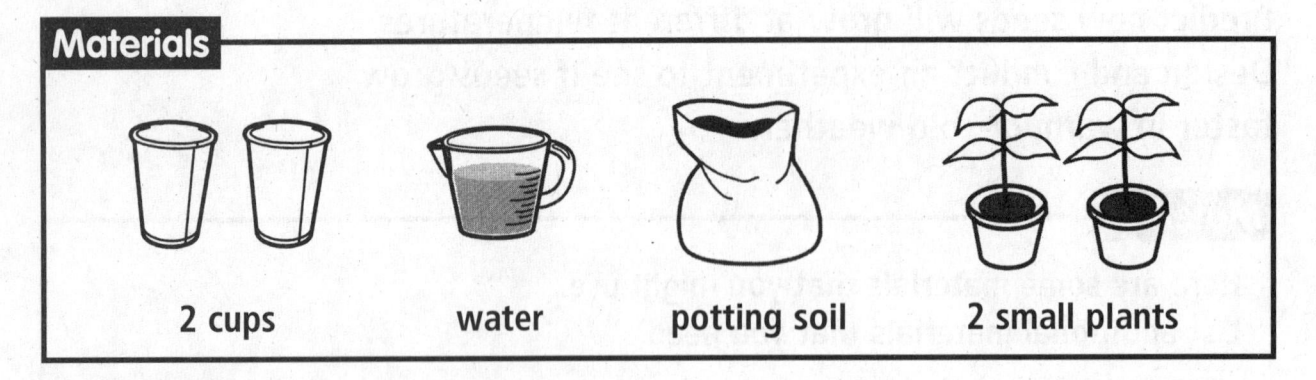

Materials

2 cups   water   potting soil   2 small plants

Procedure

1. Half-fill each cup with potting soil. Gently place a plant in each cup. Fill the cups with soil. Water each plant lightly. Use just enough water to make the soil damp.

2. Put one cup near a sunny window. Put the other cup in a dark place, such as a cabinet or closet.

3. **Observe** the cups for two weeks. Water the plants when necessary. **Record** the changes you observe. Make sure to look for changes in plant size and color.

Day	Sunny	Dark

LM 38 Lab Manual   (page 1 of 3)   Use with pages 100–101.

Name _____

Investigate Log

Draw Conclusions

1. Which plant looked healthier? How did it look different from the other plant? What do you think made this plant healthy?

   _____

   _____

   _____

2. What was different for the plant that looked less healthy?

   _____

3. **Inquiry Skill—*Compare*** Scientists often **compare** the results they get in their experiments. How would you **compare** your findings?

   _____

   _____

Inquiry Skill Tip

Organizing your observations makes it easier to compare. Make a table with a column for each object you want to **compare**. Make a row for each property you observe.

Investigate Self-Assessment	Agree	Not Sure	Disagree
I potted and watered the two plants the same way.			
I washed my hands after touching the plants and soil.			
I **compared** the plants to find out which looked healthier.			

Use with pages 100–101.   Lab Manual   LM 39

Name _____
Date _____

Investigate Log

Independent Inquiry

Predict how growing plants under different colored light might affect them. Now try it!

Materials

Here are some materials that you might use.
List additional materials that you need.

- paper cups
- water
- potting soil
- small plants
- red and green colored plastic wrap

1. Which color of light do you predict will help plants grow best? Explain.

   _____

   _____

2. Use the table below to record your observations. At the top of each column, record the color of light the plant will be under.

Day	PLANT 1 Normal Light	PLANT 2 Color of Light _____	PLANT 3 Color of Light _____
1			
5			
10			
15			
20			
25			

3. What can you conclude from the results of your investigation?

   _____

LM 40   Lab Manual

Name _____

Date _____

Investigate Log

Animal Homes

Materials

picture sorting cards · index cards · markers · reference books

Procedure

1. Look at the picture sorting cards your teacher has given you.

2. As you **observe** each picture, notice the animal's home.

3. With a partner, make a matching game. On separate index cards, write the name or draw a picture of each animal. Name or draw its home on another card. Use the picture sorting cards or reference books if you need help.

4. Play your matching game. As you match the animals to their homes, discuss the different types of homes. Talk about the ways the homes are alike and the ways they are different. Then **classify** the animals by the types of homes they live in.

Animal	Home

Use with pages 114–115.

Name _____

Investigate Log

Draw Conclusions

1. Describe the homes of the foxes and the owl. How are the homes alike? How are they different?

   _____

   _____

   _____

2. **Inquiry Skill—*Compare*** Compare two of the animal homes you observed. Explain how each home protects the animal that lives there.

   _____

   _____

   _____

Inquiry Skill Tip

When you **compare**, make a list of how the objects are alike and a separate list of how they are different. Then write a short summary of the similarities and differences.

Investigate Self-Assessment	Agree	Not Sure	Disagree
I identified the homes of different animals.			
I matched animals with their homes.			
I **compared** the characteristics of different animals' homes.			

LM 42 Lab Manual   (page 2 of 3)   Use with pages 114–115.

Name _____
Date _____

Investigate Log

Independent Inquiry

Study the animal pictures again. Draw conclusions about why each animal uses the type of home it does.

Materials

Here are some materials that you might use.
List additional materials that you need.
- reference books

1. List some different homes that animals have.

   _____

2. Use the table below to record your observations of animals' homes.

Animal	Home	Animal	Home

3. Classify the animals by their homes.

   _____

   _____

   _____

Use with page 115. Lab Manual LM 43

Name _____
Date _____

Investigate Log

Keeping Warm

Materials

- large plastic bowl
- large spoon 
- disposable plastic gloves 
- water 
- ice 
- solid vegetable shortening 
- large zip-top plastic bag 

Procedure

1. Fill the bowl with water and ice. Use the spoon to half-fill the bag with vegetable shortening.

2. Put a glove on each hand.

3. Put one of your gloved hands in the zip-top bag. Mold the vegetable shortening so that it evenly covers your hand.

4. Take your hand out of the zip-top bag, and put both hands in the water. **Compare** the way your hands feel. **Record** your **observations**.

Hand	Observations
Without shortening	
With shortening	

LM 44 Lab Manual (page 1 of 3) Use with pages 124–125.

Name _____

Investigate Log

Draw Conclusions

1. Which hand felt warmer in the ice water? Why?

   _____

   _____

2. **Inquiry Skill**—*Use Models* Scientists **use models** to study something they can't easily observe. In this Investigate, you **made a model** of a mammal with a layer of blubber, or fat. Why was making a model easier than observing the animal?

   _____

   _____

   _____

Inquiry Skill Tip

When you **make a model**, it is important that the model match as closely as possible the real-life object it represents. In this Investigate, for example, shortening is a good model for blubber because both are kinds of fat.

Investigate Self-Assessment	Agree	Not Sure	Disagree
I followed the directions for preparing an ice water bath.			
I compared how my hand felt in the ice water with and without the shortening protecting it.			
I **made a model** of a mammal with a layer of blubber.			

Use with pages 124–125.

Name _____
Date _____

Investigate Log

Independent Inquiry

How does fur protect animals from cold? Write a hypothesis. Conduct a simple investigation to find out.

Materials

Here are some materials that you might use.
List additional materials that you need.

- large plastic bowl
- disposable glove
- water
- large zip-top plastic bag
- ice

1. Write a hypothesis about how fur protects animals from the cold.

   _____
   _____
   _____

2. Draw a data table below. Use the table to record the observations you make during your investigation.

3. Use your results to infer how fur protects animals from the cold. How do your results compare with your hypothesis?

   _____
   _____
   _____

LM 46 Lab Manual   (page 3 of 3)   Use with page 125.

Name _____
Date _____

Investigate Log

A Worm Farm

Materials

- canning jar with lid
- soil
- oatmeal
- sand
- earthworms
- square of dark fabric

Procedure

1. Put 2 cm of moist soil into the jar. Sprinkle a very thin layer of oatmeal over the soil. Add 2 cm of moist sand.

2. Repeat the layers of soil, oatmeal, and sand until the jar is almost full. About 5 cm from the top, add a last layer of soil. Do not sprinkle any oatmeal on the top of the last layer. Put several worms on top of the soil.

3. Place the fabric square over the opening of the jar. Screw the lid onto the jar, or use a rubber band to hold the fabric in place. Put the jar in a dark place.

4. After one week, **observe** the jar. **Compare** the way it looks now with the way it looked when you set it up.

	Observations	Sketch of Jar
Start		
One week later		

Use with pages 136–137.   (page 1 of 3)   Lab Manual   LM 47

Name _____

Investigate Log

Draw Conclusions

1. What changes did you **observe**?

   _____

   _____

2. Inquiry Skill—*Draw a Conclusion* Draw a **conclusion** about why these changes occurred.

   _____

   _____

   _____

Inquiry Skill Tip

When you **draw a conclusion** in an investigation, you should use logic to explain facts. After you write a conclusion, ask, "Does this conclusion make sense? Does it explain the facts?"

Investigate Self-Assessment	Agree	Not Sure	Disagree
I followed the directions for layering the moist soil, oatmeal, and sand.			
I washed my hands after working with the soil and earthworms.			
I **drew a conclusion** about the changes I observed in the jar.			

LM 48   Lab Manual   (page 2 of 3)   Use with pages 136–137.

Name _____
Date _____

Investigate Log

Independent Inquiry

Predict some ways worms will affect soil in a garden. Plan and conduct a simple investigation to test your prediction.

Materials

Here are some materials that you might use. List additional materials that you need.

- large canning jar with ring lid
- square of dark fabric
- earthworms
- soil
- sand

1. Predict some ways worms might affect soil in a garden.

   _____
   _____
   _____

2. Choose one prediction. Describe why you think it might be true.

   _____
   _____
   _____

3. How would you conduct a simple investigation to test it?

   _____
   _____
   _____

Use with page 137.

Name _____
Date _____

Unit Inquiry Log

Unit B

Changing Environments

1. **Observe and Ask Questions**

   Throughout the year the weather changes. Most plants and animals are adapted to live in a certain climate. What happens to living things when an environment changes? Make a list of questions you have about changing environments. Then circle a question you want to investigate.

   _____

2. **Form a Hypothesis**

   Write a hypothesis. A hypothesis is a suggested answer to the question you are testing.

   _____

3. **Plan an Experiment**

   Identify and Control Variables

   To plan your experiment, you must first identify the important variables. Complete the statements below.

   The variable I will change is

   _____.

   The variables I will observe or measure are

   _____.

   The variables I will keep the same, or *control*, are

   _____.

LM 50 Lab Manual   (page 1 of 4)   Use with page 151.

Name _____

Unit Inquiry Log

Develop a Procedure and Gather Materials Write the steps you will follow to set up an experiment and collect data.

_____

_____

_____

_____

_____

_____

_____

Use extra sheets of blank paper if you need to write down more steps.

Materials List Look carefully at all the steps of your procedure, and list all the materials you will use. Be sure that your teacher approves your plan and your materials list before you begin.

_____

_____

_____

_____

Use with page 151.

Name _____

Unit Inquiry Log

4. Conduct the Experiment

Gather and Record Data Follow your plan and collect data. Use the chart below or a chart you design to record your data. **Observe** carefully. **Record** your observations and be sure to note anything unusual or unexpected.

Data for Changing Habitat					
	Day 3	Day 5	Day 7	Day 9	Day 11
Number of Plants					
Height of tallest plant					
Number of species					
Appearance of plants					
	Day 13	Day 15	Day 17	Day 19	Day 21
Number of Plants					
Height of tallest plant					
Number of species					
Appearance of plants					

Data for Habitat That Does Not Change					
	Day 3	Day 5	Day 7	Day 9	Day 11
Number of Plants					
Height of tallest plant					
Number of species					
Appearance of plants					
	Day 13	Day 15	Day 17	Day 19	Day 21
Number of Plants					
Height of tallest plant					
Number of species					
Appearance of plants					

LM 52   Lab Manual   (page 3 of 4)   Use with page 151.

Name _____

Unit Inquiry Log

Interpret Data Make graphs of the data you have collected. Plot the data on a sheet of graph paper or use a software program.

5. **Draw Conclusions and Communicate Results**

   Compare the **hypothesis** with the data and the graphs. Then answer these questions.

   1. Given the results of the experiment, do you think the hypothesis was correct? Explain.

   _____

   _____

   2. How would you revise the hypothesis? Explain.

   _____

   _____

   3. What else did you **observe** during the experiment?

   _____

   _____

Prepare a presentation for your classmates to **communicate** what you have learned. Display your data tables and graphs.

Investigate Further

Write another hypothesis that you might investigate.

_____

_____

Use with page 151.

Name _____
Date _____

Investigate Log

Observe an Environment

Materials

safety goggles

wire coat hanger

Procedure

1. **CAUTION:** Put on safety goggles. Bend the coat hanger into a square. Ask your teacher for help if necessary.

2. Go outside. Place the square on the ground. Closely **observe** the ground inside the square. This square of ground is an environment.

3. **Record** all the living things you **observe** and how many there are of each. Then **record** all the nonliving things you **observe** and how many there are of each.

4. Share your table with a classmate. **Compare** the environments you **observed.** How are they alike? How are they different?

Living Things	Number	Nonliving Things	Number

Name _____

Investigate Log

Draw Conclusions

1. **Compare** the things you found in your environment with the things a classmate found. Why do you think you found different things?

   _____

   _____

2. **Inquiry Skill—*Infer*** How did you **infer** which things were living and which things were nonliving?

   _____

   _____

Inquiry Skill Tip

Before you **infer**, define any important terms. In this Investigate, for example, you must understand what *living* and *nonliving* mean before you can infer which things fit in each category.

Investigate Self-Assessment	Agree	Not Sure	Disagree
I counted the number of living and nonliving things.			
I followed safety guidelines by wearing goggles.			
I **inferred** which things were living and which things were nonliving in the environment.			

Use with pages 156–157.

Name _____
Date _____

Investigate Log

Independent Inquiry

Compare the environment you observed at school with an environment you observe at or near your home.

Materials

Here are some materials that you might use.
List additional materials that you need.

- safety goggles
- wire coat hanger

1. What will you observe and compare in your investigation?

   _____

   _____

2. Use the table below to record your observations of an environment at or near your home.

Living Things	Number	Nonliving Things	Number

3. Compare the environment you observed at school to the environment you observed near your home.

   _____

   _____

   _____

LM 56 Lab Manual (page 3 of 3) Use with page 157.

Name _____

Date _____

Investigate Log

Grass Roots

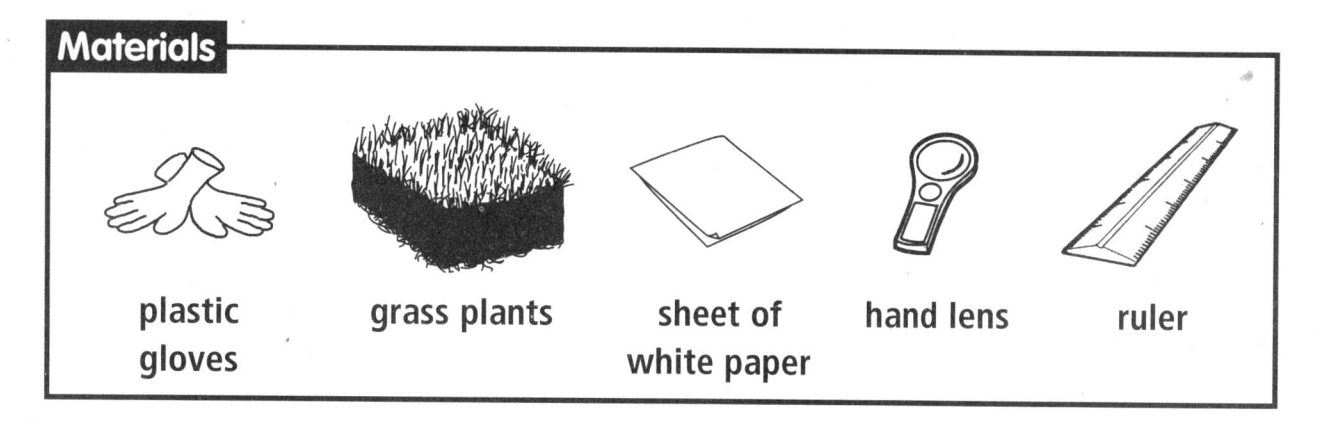

Materials

plastic gloves | grass plants | sheet of white paper | hand lens | ruler

Procedure

1. Put on the plastic gloves. **Observe** the different types of grass plants that your teacher has for you.

2. The leaves of a grass plant are called blades. Carefully hold up one grass plant by its blades. Gently shake the plant. **Observe** what happens to the soil.

3. Very carefully remove the soil from around the roots.

4. Place the grass plant on a sheet of white paper. **Observe** it with the hand lens.

5. **Measure** and **record** the height of the tallest blade and the length of the longest root.

Height of Tallest Blade	Length of Longest Root

Use with pages 166–167.   (page 1 of 3)   Lab Manual   LM 57

Name _____

Investigate Log

Draw Conclusions

1. **Compare** the height of the tallest blade with the length of the longest root.

   _____

   _____

2. **Inquiry Skill—*Infer*** Infer how the roots of a tree might be different from the roots of a grass plant.

   _____

   _____

Inquiry Skill Tip

Collect and analyze as much data as you can before you **infer**. Look for patterns in the data that might help you infer about a new situation.

Investigate Self-Assessment	Agree	Not Sure	Disagree
I observed the leaves and roots of a grass plant.			
I used the ruler to measure the tallest blade of grass and the longest root.			
I **inferred** how the roots of a tree might be different from the roots of a grass plant.			

LM 58   Lab Manual   (page 2 of 3)   Use with pages 166–167.

Name _____
Date _____

Investigate Log

Independent Inquiry

Carefully remove a plant from a pot or the ground. Compare the roots of a grass plant with the roots of the plant you have chosen.

Materials

Here are some materials that you might use.
List additional materials that you need.
- grass plants
- sheet of white paper
- potted plant or plant from the ground
- ruler
- hand lens
- plastic gloves

1. What will you observe in your investigation?

   _____
   _____

2. Compare the roots of the grass plant to the roots of the plant you chose.

   _____
   _____
   _____

3. What can you conclude about the relationship between the size of a plant and the size of its roots?

   _____
   _____
   _____

Use with page 167.   Lab Manual

Name _____
Date _____

Investigate Log

How Insects Hide

Materials

- construction paper
- ruler
- crayons or markers
- chenille sticks
- scissors
- tape
- watch or clock

Procedure

1. Look around the classroom for a "habitat" for a model insect you will make. **Observe** the colors and shapes of things in the habitat.

2. Draw a construction-paper rectangle 5 cm long and 3 cm wide. This will be the size of your insect.

3. Color the body so your insect blends into its habitat. Make legs and wings.

4. Tape your insect in its habitat. Don't hide it behind anything.

5. Ask a classmate to be a "bird." Ask the bird to look for the insect and other classmates' insects for one minute. **Record** the results in a table. Give the bird another minute. **Record** the results. Continue until the bird finds all the insects.

Minute	Number of Insects Found	Description of Insects Found
1		
2		
3		
4		
5		

LM 60   Lab Manual   (page 1 of 3)   Use with pages 176–177.

Name _____

Investigate Log

Draw Conclusions

1. Which insects did the bird find first? Why were they easy to find?

   _____

   _____

   _____

2. **Inquiry Skill—*Infer*** Infer why some insects were hard to find.

   _____

   _____

   _____

Inquiry Skill Tip

The word **infer** comes from the Latin word *inferre* which means "to bring in." Use this meaning to remind you to "bring in" as much information as possible before you infer.

Investigate Self-Assessment	Agree	Not Sure	Disagree
I followed the directions for making an insect.			
I used the ruler to measure the insect's body.			
I **inferred** why some insects were hard to find.			

Use with pages 176–177.

Name _____

Date _____

Investigate Log

Independent Inquiry

Draw conclusions about why the fur of some animals, such as foxes and rabbits, changes color with the seasons.

Materials

Here are some materials that you might use.
List additional materials that you need.

- reference books

1. Choose an animal that has fur that changes with the seasons. Research its summer and winter environments and identify the color of its fur in both seasons.

   _____
   _____
   _____
   _____

2. What similarities are there between the animal's fur color and its environments?

   _____
   _____

3. Why do you think the animal's fur changes color with the seasons?

   _____
   _____

LM 62 Lab Manual (page 3 of 3) Use with page 177.

Name _____

Date _____

Investigate Log

Changing the Environment

Materials

- moist sand
- shallow cardboard box
- leaves and twigs
- wooden block
- water
- watering can
- small stones

Procedure

1. With a partner, pack the sand into the box. Use your fingers to make hills, valleys, and a streambed. Push the leaves and twigs into the sand to represent plants.

2. Carefully lift one end of the box off the table. Place the wooden block beneath that end.

3. Slowly pour a little water from the watering can into the streambed you made. **Observe** and **record** what happens to the sand, water, and plants.

4. Pour the water more quickly into the streambed, and **observe** and **record** again.

Observations (slow water)	Observations (fast water)

Use with pages 186–187.   (page 1 of 3)   Lab Manual   **LM 63**

Name _____

Investigate Log

Draw Conclusions

1. What happens to the sand, water, and plants when only a little water is poured into the streambed?

   _____

   _____

2. **Inquiry Skill—*Predict*** Add several stones along the streambed. **Predict** what will happen if you pour a lot of water into the streambed. Try it. Was your prediction correct?

   _____

   _____

> **Inquiry Skill Tip**
>
> A good **prediction** is based on past observations, measurements, and data. If you can explain why you think a prediction will be true, then it is a good prediction—whether it turns out to be correct or not.

Investigate Self-Assessment	Agree	Not Sure	Disagree
I built an environment with sand, twigs and leaves.			
I washed my hands after working with the sand, leaves, and twigs.			
I **predicted** what would happen after I added stones along the streambed in the box.			

LM 64 Lab Manual   (page 2 of 3)   Use with pages 186–187.

Name _____
Date _____

Investigate Log

Independent Inquiry

Predict what will happen to the sand, plants, and water if you make a dam across your streambed. Try it.

Materials

Here are some materials that you might use.
List additional materials that you need.
- shallow cardboard box
- moist sand
- water
- leaves and twigs
- wooden block
- watering can

1. Predict what will happen if you make a dam across your streambed.

   _____
   _____

2. Build a model with a dam, and then add the water. What did you observe?

   _____
   _____
   _____

3. Did the results of your investigation support your prediction? What does the model show about the effects of a dam on an environment?

   _____
   _____
   _____

Use with page 187.   (page 3 of 3)   Lab Manual   LM 65

Name _____

Date _____

Investigate Log

Checking Teeth

Materials

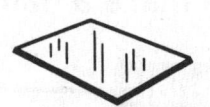

paper and pencil | picture sorting cards | small mirror

Procedure

1. Use the table below for this investigation.
2. **Observe** the picture sorting cards that your teacher has provided.
3. On your table, **record** the name of an animal. Draw the shape of its teeth. It might have teeth of different shapes.
4. **Record** words that describe the teeth.
5. Read the back of the picture sorting card. **Record** the foods the animal eats.
6. Repeat Steps 2–5 for four other animals.
7. Use the mirror to **observe** your own teeth. Add yourself to the table.

Kind of Animal	Drawing of Teeth	Description of Teeth	Kinds of Food

LM 66   Lab Manual   (page 1 of 3)   Use with pages 200–201.

Name _____

Investigate Log

Draw Conclusions

1. Which of the animals in your table catch other animals for food? Which of the animals eat plants?

_____

_____

Inquiry Skill Tip

To help you **infer**, start by making a list of all your observations.

2. Inquiry Skill—*Infer* Scientists learn by **observing**. Then they use what they **observe** to **infer** the reasons for something. What can you **infer** about the shape of an animal's teeth and the kind of food it eats?

_____

_____

_____

Investigate Self-Assessment	Agree	Not Sure	Disagree
I observed the picture cards and my own teeth according to the directions for this investigation.			
I placed all my observations in the table.			
I **made an inference** about the ways animals use their teeth.			

Use with page 200–201. (page 2 of 3) Lab Manual **LM 67**

Name _____
Date _____

Investigate Log

Independent Inquiry

Choose another animal. Find out what it eats and predict what kind of teeth it has. Then find out if you are correct.

Materials

Here are some materials that you might use. List additional materials that you need.

- paper and pencil
- picture sorting cards

1. What do you predict about the teeth of the animal you chose?

   _____

   _____

   _____

2. Use this table to record your data.

Kind of Animal	Kinds of Food Eaten	Prediction: kind of teeth	Actual kind of teeth

3. Explain how the outcome of your investigation compares to your prediction.

   _____

   _____

   _____

LM 68 Lab Manual   (page 3 of 3)   Use with page 201.

Name _____

Date _____

Investigate Log

Making a Food Chain

Materials

5 index cards   marker   4 pieces of string or yarn   tape

Procedure

1. Number the index cards 1 through 5 in the bottom right-hand corner.

2. On Card 1, draw and label grass. Draw and label a cricket on Card 2. On Card 3, draw and label a frog. Draw and label a snake on Card 4. On Card 5, draw and label a hawk.

3. Put the cards in order by number. Use the yarn and the tape to connect them.

4. Lay the connected cards on a table. You have **made a model** of a food chain!

Organism	What It Eats	What Eats It

Use with pages 210–211.   Lab Manual

Name _____

Investigate Log

Draw Conclusions

1. Which part of your food chain is a producer? Which parts are consumers?

   _____

   _____

2. **Inquiry Skill—*Make a Model*** Scientists **make a model** to study and understand a process. How does the **model** you made help you understand food chains?

   _____

   _____

   _____

Inquiry Skill Tip

Some models have many parts. When you **make a model**, make sure that all the parts work together to get your idea across.

Investigate Self-Assessment	Agree	Not Sure	Disagree
I made a food chain according to the directions for this investigation.			
I put away any leftover materials when I finished the investigation.			
I **made a model** of a food chain and used it to see relationships between living things.			

LM 70   Lab Manual   (page 2 of 3)   Use with pages 210–211.

Name _____
Date _____

Investigate Log

Independent Inquiry

Find out what some other kinds of organisms eat. Make a model that shows the relationship between a producer and some consumers.

Materials

Here are some materials that you might use.
List additional materials that you need.

- 5 index cards
- marker
- 4 pieces of string or yarn
- tape

1. What will your model show about the animals you have chosen?

   _____
   _____
   _____

2. Make a diagram of the food chain model you made.

3. How is this food chain different from the one you made in the Investigate?

   _____
   _____
   _____

Use with page 211.

Name _____
Date _____

Investigate Log

Making a Food Web

Materials

- index cards, cut into fourths
- poster board
- tape or glue
- crayons

Procedure

1. Write the name of each living thing from the table shown in your textbook on its own card.

2. Tape or glue the cards in a circle on the poster board.

3. Use the table to make two different food chains. **Record** them in the space below.

4. Use a crayon to draw arrows between the parts of one food chain. Use a different color to draw arrows between the parts of the other food chain.

5. **Observe** where the food chains overlap. You just **made a model** of a food web.

Living Thing	How Many It Eats	How Many Eat It
clover		
grasshopper		
frog		
snake		
owl		
mouse		

LM 72 Lab Manual   Use with pages 220–221.

Name _____

Investigate Log

Draw Conclusions

1. Why should both your food chains start with clover?

   _____

   _____

2. **Inquiry Skill—*Communicate*** Scientists often use models, graphs, and drawings to **communicate** ideas. How does your model help **communicate** what a food web is?

   _____

   _____

   _____

> **Inquiry Skill Tip**
>
> You have many ways to **communicate**. When you have an idea you want to share, decide whether writing, speaking, or using pictures or diagrams will work best.

Investigate Self-Assessment	Agree	Not Sure	Disagree
I used the materials to make a food web according to the directions for this investigation.			
I cleaned up after I finished using the glue.			
I used my model food chain to **communicate** the relationships between animals.			

Use with pages 220–221. (page 2 of 3) **Lab Manual** LM 73

Name _____
Date _____

Investigate Log

Independent Inquiry

Choose an animal you like. Find out what it eats and what eats it. Then make a model of a food web that includes this animal.

Materials

Here are some materials that you might use.
List additional materials that you need.

- index cards, cut into fourths
- poster board
- tape or glue
- crayons

1. What are the animals that you are including in your food web?

_____
_____
_____

2. Use this space to draw your food web. Label the plants and animals.

3. How is a food web different from a food chain?

_____
_____
_____

Name _____
Date _____

Unit Inquiry Log
Unit C

Hurricane Damage

1. Observe and Ask Questions

Hurricanes have winds of at least 74 miles per hour (119 kilometers per hour). Why are some structures damaged during a hurricane while others are not? Make a list of questions you have about wind damage in a hurricane. Then circle a question to investigate.

_____

2. Form a Hypothesis

Write a hypothesis. A hypothesis is a suggested answer to the question you are testing.

_____

3. Plan an Experiment

Identify and Control Variables

To plan your experiment, you must first identify the important variables. Complete the statements below.

The variable I will change is

_____.

The variables I will observe or measure are

_____.

The variables I will keep the same, or *control*, are

_____.

Use with page 241. (page 1 of 4) Lab Manual LM 75

Name _____

Unit Inquiry Log

Develop a Procedure and Gather Materials Write the steps you will follow to set up an experiment and collect data.

_____
_____
_____
_____
_____
_____
_____

Use extra sheets of blank paper if you need to write down more steps.

Materials List Look carefully at all the steps of your procedure, and list all the materials you will use. Be sure that your teacher approves your plan and your materials list before you begin.

_____
_____
_____
_____
_____

LM 76 Lab Manual (page 2 of 4) Use with page 241.

Name _____

Unit Inquiry Log

4. Conduct the Experiment

Gather and Record Data Follow your plan and collect data. Use the table below or a table you design to record your data. **Observe** carefully. **Record** your observations and be sure to note anything unusual or unexpected.

	Building Height (cm)	Building Width (cm)	Distance Between Hair Dryer and Damaged Building (cm)
1.			
2.			
3.			
4.			
5.			
6.			
7.			
8.			
9.			
10.			
11.			
12.			

Use with page 241.

Name _____

Unit Inquiry Log

Interpret Data Make graphs of the data you have collected. Plot the data on a sheet of graph paper or use a software program.

5. **Draw Conclusions and Communicate Results**

   Compare the **hypothesis** with the data and the graphs. Then answer these questions.

   1. Given the results of the experiment, do you think the hypothesis was correct? Explain.

      _____
      _____

   2. How would you revise the hypothesis? Explain.

      _____
      _____

   3. What else did you **observe** during the experiment?

      _____
      _____

Prepare a presentation for your classmates to **communicate** what you have learned. Display your data tables and graphs.

Investigate Further

Write another hypothesis that you might investigate.

_____
_____

LM 78 Lab Manual   (page 4 of 4)   Use with page 241.

Name _____

Date _____

Investigate Log

Testing Minerals

Materials

- safety goggles
- Minerals Labeled A through G

Procedure

1. Make a table like the one shown.

2. **CAUTION:** Put on safety goggles. A harder mineral scratches a softer mineral. Try to scratch each mineral with Sample A. **Record** which minerals Sample A scratches.

3. A softer mineral can be scratched by a harder mineral. Try to scratch Sample A with each of the other minerals. **Record** the minerals that scratch Sample A.

4. Repeat Steps 2 and 3 for each mineral.

5. Using the information in your table, **order** the minerals from softest to hardest.

Mineral to Test	Minerals It Scratches	Minerals That Scratch It
Sample A		
Sample B		
Sample C		
Sample D		
Sample E		
Sample F		
Sample G		

Use with pages 246–247.

Name _____

Investigate Log

Draw Conclusions

1. Which mineral is the hardest? Which is the softest? How do you know?

   _____

   _____

   _____

2. **Inquiry Skill—*Order*** Scientists often put objects in **order**. How did you decide how to **order** the minerals? How can putting minerals in **order** of hardness help you identify them?

   _____

   _____

   _____

Inquiry Skill Tip

To put a series of objects in **order**, begin by placing two objects in order. Then fit another object into the sequence. Continue, adding one object at a time.

Investigate Self-Assessment	Agree	Not Sure	Disagree
I tested each mineral according to the directions for this investigation.			
I wore my safety goggles throughout the investigation.			
I put the minerals in **order** based on their hardness.			

LM 80 Lab Manual (page 2 of 3) Use with pages 246–247.

Name _____
Date _____

Investigate Log

Independent Inquiry

Test the hardness of each mineral again. This time, use a penny and your fingernail. Classify the minerals by what scratches them.

Materials

Here are some materials that you might use.
List additional materials that you need.

- safety goggles
- minerals labeled A through G
- penny

1. What are you trying to find out by scratching the minerals with a penny and with your fingernail?

   _____

   _____

2. Use this table to record your data.

Mineral to Test	Can be scratched by a penny	Can be scratched by a fingernail
Sample A		
Sample B		
Sample C		
Sample D		
Sample E		
Sample F		
Sample G		

3. Which mineral is harder: one that can be scratched by a penny but not a fingernail, or one that can be scratched by a fingernail? Explain.

   _____

   _____

Use with page 247.   Lab Manual

Name _____
Date _____

Investigate Log

Make a Model Rock

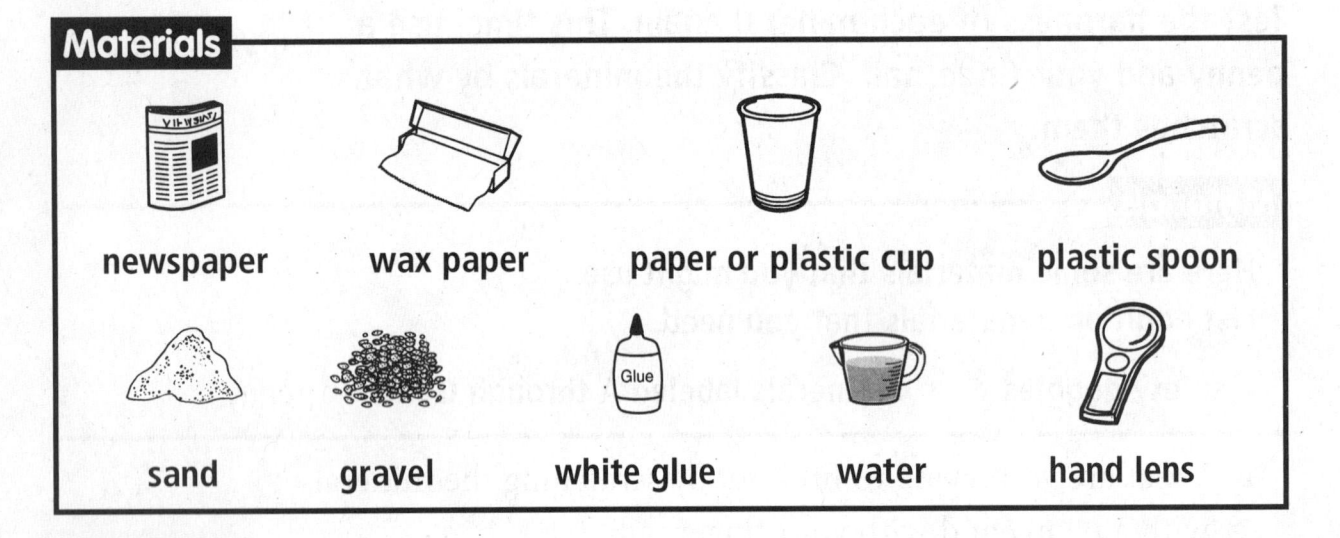

Materials

- newspaper
- wax paper
- paper or plastic cup
- plastic spoon
- sand
- gravel
- white glue
- water
- hand lens

Procedure

1. Spread newspaper over your work area. Place a smaller sheet of wax paper on the newspaper.
2. Place 1 spoonful of sand in the cup.
3. Add 1 spoonful of gravel to the cup. Stir the sand and gravel.
4. Add 1 spoonful of glue to the cup.
5. Stir the mixture until it forms a lump. You may need to add a little water.
6. Pour the mixture onto the wax paper, and let it dry. You have made a **model** of a rock.

Property	Observation
Color	
Texture	
Hardness	
Drawing of Rock	

LM 82 Lab Manual   (page 1 of 3)   Use with pages 256–257.

Name _____

Investigate Log

Draw Conclusions

1. Use the hand lens to **observe** the dried mixture you made. What does the mixture look like?

   _____

   _____

2. **Inquiry Skill—***Use Models* Scientists often **use models** to understand processes they can't easily observe. One way rocks can form is when sand and gravel are somehow cemented or glued together. How is the **model** you made like a rock?

   _____

   _____

   _____

Inquiry Skill Tip

When you can **use a model** to make observations, make a list of ways you can compare the model and the actual object.

Investigate Self-Assessment	Agree	Not Sure	Disagree
I used the materials to make a rock model according to the directions for this investigation.			
I washed my hands after working with the sand, gravel, and glue.			
I **used the model** of a rock to make observations.			

Use with pages 256–257. (page 2 of 3) Lab Manual LM 83

Name _____
Date _____

Investigate Log

Independent Inquiry

Make models of rocks by using different materials. Explore how changing the materials changes the rock.

Materials

Here are some materials that you might use.
List additional materials that you need.

- newspaper
- plastic spoon
- white glue
- wax paper
- sand
- water
- paper or plastic cup
- gravel
- hand lens

1. Describe how you will make your models of rocks.

   _____
   _____
   _____

2. Use this space to describe your rock models.

	Materials used to make model	Description of model
Model #1		
Model #2		
Model #3		

3. Compare your rock models to each other. How do the materials change the nature of each model?

   _____
   _____
   _____

LM 84   Lab Manual   Use with page 257.

Name _____

Date _____

Investigate Log

Make a Model Fossil

Materials

seashell | petroleum jelly | modeling clay | small bowl or paper plate | white glue

Procedure

1. Coat the outside of the seashell with a thin layer of petroleum jelly.

2. Press the seashell into the clay to **make a model** of a fossil.

3. Remove the seashell carefully from the clay.

4. Place the clay with the seashell's shape in the plastic bowl.

5. Drizzle white glue into the imprint. Fill it completely. This also **makes a model** of a fossil.

6. Let the glue harden for about a day. When it is hard, separate the hardened glue from the clay

Kind of Fossil	Description
Modeling Clay Fossil	
Glue Fossil	

Use with pages 268–269. (page 1 of 3) Lab Manual LM 85

Name _____

Investigate Log

Draw Conclusions

1. You made two **models** of fossils. How do the fossils compare?

   _____
   _____
   _____

2. **Inquiry Skill**—*Use Models* Scientists **use models** to better understand how things happen. How do you think pressing the seashell into the clay models how a fossil forms?

   _____
   _____
   _____

Inquiry Skill Tip

When you **use a model**, you can make many kinds of observations. You can observe how the model looks and how the model was made. Compare these observations to the real object's appearance and the way it formed.

Investigate Self-Assessment	Agree	Not Sure	Disagree
I used the materials to make fossil models according to the directions for this investigation.			
I washed my hands after using the materials.			
I **used the models** to make observations about fossils.			

LM 86   Lab Manual   (page 2 of 3)   Use with pages 268–269.

Name _____

Date _____

Investigate Log

Independent Inquiry

Use at least four other once-living materials such as fallen leaves to make models of fossils. Which materials make the best fossils?

Materials

Here are some materials that you might use. List additional materials that you need.

- petroleum jelly
- small plastic bowl
- modeling clay
- white glue
- fallen leaves

1. What kinds of materials will you use to make your fossil models?

   _____

   _____

2. Make a drawing of each fossil model you make. Label it to show what kind of fossil it is.

Fossil #1	Fossil #2	Fossil #3	Fossil #4

3. Compare the different once-living materials you used and tell which make the best fossils. What can you infer about how well fossils form from different kinds of animals and plants?

   _____

   _____

   _____

Use with page 269.

Name _____

Date _____

Investigate Log

Folds in Earth's Crust

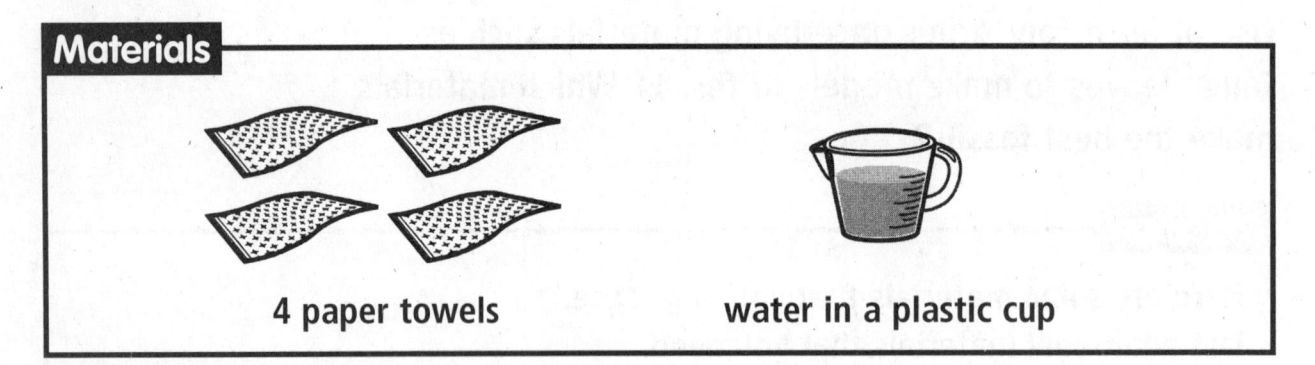

Materials

4 paper towels

water in a plastic cup

Procedure

1. Stack the paper towels on a table. Fold the stack in half.
2. Sprinkle water on both sides of the towels. They should be damp but not very wet.
3. Place your hands on the ends of the damp towels.
4. Slowly push the ends toward the center. **Record** your **observations.**

	Observations	Sketch of Towels
Before pushing		
After pushing		

Name _____

Investigate Log

Draw Conclusions

1. What happened as you pushed the edges of the towels together?

   _____

   _____

2. How did the height of the towels change as you pushed them?

   _____

   _____

3. **Inquiry Skill**—*Use Models* Scientists **use models** to understand how things happen. How does this model help you understand how some mountains form?

   _____

   _____

   _____

Inquiry Skill Tip

When you **use a model**, identify what each part of the model represents. In this Investigate, the paper towels represent layers of rocks. The water helps the paper towels fold the way real rock layers do.

Investigate Self-Assessment	Agree	Not Sure	Disagree
I made a stack of damp paper towels.			
I pushed the stack at the edges.			
I **used a model** to understand how rock layers can form mountains.			

Use with pages 284–285.   Lab Manual LM 89

Name _____
Date _____

Investigate Log

Independent Inquiry

Other mountains form when two sections of Earth's crust push against each other. How would you use a model to show this?

Materials

Here are some materials that you might use.
List additional materials that you need.

- 4 paper towels
- water in a plastic cup

1. What materials will represent the two pieces of Earth's crust in your model?

   _____

   _____

2. Make a model to show how mountains can form when two pieces of Earth's crust push together. Describe your results.

   _____

   _____

   _____

   _____

3. Explain what the model shows about how Earth's crust forms mountains.

   _____

   _____

   _____

LM 90   Lab Manual   (page 3 of 3)   Use with page 285.

Name _____
Date _____

Investigate Log

Water at Work

Materials

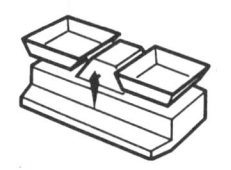

balance 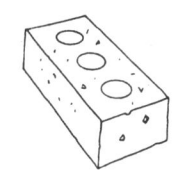 | small pieces of brick  | clear jar with lid  | water 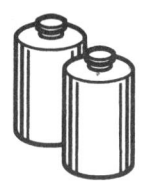 | extra masses for the balance

Procedure

1. **Measure** the mass of the brick pieces. **Record** your results.

2. Fill the jar three-fourths full with water.

3. Put the brick pieces into the jar of water. Put the lid on the jar.

4. Take turns with a partner to shake the jar for 10 minutes. Do this three times a day for one week.

5. After one week, take the brick pieces out of the jar, and let them dry. **Measure** the mass of the brick pieces. **Record** your results.

Time	Mass of Brick Pieces
Day 1	
1 week later	

Use with pages 294–295.   (page 1 of 3)   Lab Manual   LM 91

Name _____

Investigate Log

Draw Conclusions

1. Do the brick pieces look different after a week of shaking them? If so, how are they different?

   _____

   _____

   _____

2. **Compare** the mass of the brick pieces before and after the shaking. Did the mass of the brick pieces change? If so, how did it change?

   _____

3. Inquiry Skill—*Interpret Data* Scientists **interpret data** to understand how things work. Use your data to tell what happened to the brick pieces.

   _____

   _____

> **Inquiry Skill Tip**
>
> When you **interpret data**, you explain the results you collected in an investigation. To do this, think about your data and observation. Then give a reason for what happened.

Investigate Self-Assessment	Agree	Not Sure	Disagree
I followed the instructions for this investigation.			
I used the balance to measure the mass of the brick pieces before and after the investigation.			
I **interpreted the data** to explain changes in the brick pieces.			

LM 92 Lab Manual   Use with pages 294–295.

Name _____

Date _____

Investigate Log

Independent Inquiry

Do large pieces of rock weather faster than small ones?
Plan and conduct an investigation to test your prediction.

Materials

Here are some materials that you might use.
List additional materials that you need.

- balance
- large pieces of brick
- clear jar with lid
- water
- extra masses for the balance
- small pieces of brick

1. Predict whether larger or smaller rock pieces will weather faster. Explain your prediction.

   _____
   _____
   _____
   _____

2. Conduct your investigation. Make a table to organize your results.

3. Do the results of the investigation agree with your prediction? Explain.

   _____
   _____
   _____
   _____

Use with page 295.   Lab Manual   LM 93

Name _____
Date _____

Investigate Log

A Model Volcano

Materials

- large tray
- wax paper
- measuring spoons
- water
- red and green food coloring
- flour
- 2 plastic jars
- baking soda
- measuring cup
- lab apron
- safety goggles
- soil
- white vinegar

Procedure

1. **CAUTION: Put on safety goggles and a lab apron.** Cover the tray with wax paper. Put one jar in the middle of the tray.

2. Mix $\frac{1}{2}$ tsp flour and 1 tsp baking soda in the jar. Add 10 drops of red food coloring.

3. Dampen the soil a little, and pack it in a cone shape around the jar. Make the top of the soil even with the top of the jar.

4. Slowly pour $\frac{1}{4}$ cup vinegar into the jar. **Observe** what happens. Remove the jar carefully. Wait 15 minutes.

5. Repeat Steps 2 through 4 with green food coloring and the other jar. **Record** your **observations.**

Color	Observations
Red	
Green	

LM 94 Lab Manual   (page 1 of 3)   Use with pages 304–305.

Name _____

Investigate Log

Draw Conclusions

1. What happened when you poured the vinegar into the jar? What does the mixture represent?

   _____
   _____
   _____

2. **Inquiry Skill—*Use Models*** Scientists **use models** to understand how things happen in nature. How did your model help you learn how volcanoes change the land?

   _____
   _____
   _____

Inquiry Skill Tip

It is a good idea to **use a model** when actual events occur too slowly or quickly to see. You can also use a model when events are too dangerous to observe in nature.

Investigate Self-Assessment	Agree	Not Sure	Disagree
I followed the directions for this investigation.			
I wore safety goggles and a lab apron.			
I **made a model** to understand how volcanoes might change the land.			

Use with pages 304–305.   Lab Manual

Name _____
Date _____

Investigate Log

Independent Inquiry

Learn about different types of volcanic eruptions. Choose one type. Plan and conduct an investigation to model it.

Materials

Here are some materials that you might use.
List additional materials that you need.

- safety goggles
- large tray
- water
- measuring spoons
- red and green food coloring
- baking soda
- soil
- 3 plastic jars
- white vinegar
- lab apron
- wax paper
- measuring cup
- flour

1. Describe at least two different kinds of eruptions.

   _____
   _____

2. Describe the model you made for one type of eruption.

   _____
   _____

3. Describe why the mixture you used to model magma produced the type of eruption you observed.

   _____
   _____
   _____

LM 96 Lab Manual Use with page 305.

Name _____

Date _____

Investigate Log

Mining Resources

Materials

oatmeal-raisin cookie   dropper   water   paper plate   toothpick

Procedure

1 **Observe** your cookie. **Record** the number of raisins you see.

2 Put a few drops of water around each raisin. The cookie should be moist but not wet.

3 Use the toothpick to "mine" all the raisins from the cookie. If they are hard to get out, put a few more drops of water around them. Put the removed raisins on the plate. **Record** the number of raisins you removed.

Raisins Observed in Step 1	Total Number of Raisins Counted

Draw Conclusions

1. Were there any raisins that you didn't see in the cookie the first time? Why didn't you see them?

   _____

2. How did the water help you dig out the raisins? How did the digging affect the cookie?

   _____

   _____

Use with pages 320–321.   (page 1 of 3)   Lab Manual   LM 97

Name _____

Investigate Log

3. How is "mining" raisins from a cookie like mining resources from Earth?

_____

_____

Inquiry Skill Tip

To help you **infer**, start by making a list of all your **observations**.

4. Inquiry Skill—*Infer* Scientists use their **observations** to **infer** how similar things work. Use your observations to **infer** how mining could affect the land around the mine.

_____

_____

_____

Investigate Self-Assessment	Agree	Not Sure	Disagree
I followed the directions for modeling the way resources are mined.			
I obeyed safety rules by not placing any materials used in the investigation into my mouth.			
I **made an inference** about how mining could affect the land around the mine.			

LM 98   Lab Manual   (page 2 of 3)   Use with pages 320–321.

Name _____

Date _____

Investigate Log

Independent Inquiry

Can the cookie be completely "mined" without tearing it up? Hypothesize how this might be done. Test your hypothesis.

Materials

Here are some materials that you might use.
List additional materials that you need.

- oatmeal-raisin cookie
- dropper
- water
- paper plate
- toothpick

1. Write a hypothesis for your investigation.

   _____

   _____

2. Describe your observations as you "mine" the cookie.

   _____

   _____

   _____

   _____

3. Did the investigation support your hypothesis? Explain.

   _____

   _____

   _____

   _____

Use with page 321.   (page 3 of 3)   Lab Manual   LM 99

Name _____
Date _____

Investigate Log

Observing Soil

Materials

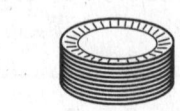

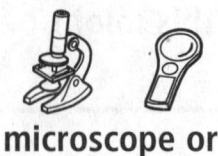

- 2 soil samples
- small paper plates
- microscope or hand lens
- toothpick

Procedure

1. Get a soil sample from your teacher. Place some of the soil on a paper plate.

2. Using the microscope or hand lens, **observe** the soil. Use the toothpick to move the soil grains around. Notice the colors, shapes, and sizes of the grains. **Record** what you **observe** by drawing the soil grains.

3. Pick up some soil from the plate. Rub it between your fingers. How does it feel? **Record** what you **observe**.

4. Repeat Steps 1 through 3 with the other soil sample.

Drawings

Sample 1	Sample 2

Characteristic	Sample 1 _____	Sample 2 _____
color		
shape		
size		
feel		

LM 100 Lab Manual (page 1 of 3) Use with pages 330–331.

Name _____

Investigate Log

Draw Conclusions

1. What senses did you use to **observe** the soil?

   _____

2. Describe your **observations**.

   _____

   _____

3. **Inquiry Skill—*Observe*** Scientists **observe** things so they can **compare** them. How were the soil samples alike? How were the soil samples different?

   _____

   _____

   _____

Inquiry Skill Tip

The **observations** you make during an investigation aren't just the things you can see. They involve different senses, but the senses you use will depend on the type of investigation. The senses of smell, sight, touch, and hearing often give important information.

Investigate Self-Assessment	Agree	Not Sure	Disagree
I followed the directions for this investigation.			
I used the toothpick to move the soil grains around.			
I was able to **observe** how the soils were alike and how they were different.			

Use with pages 330–331. (page 2 of 3) Lab Manual LM 101

Name _____
Date _____

Investigate Log

Independent Inquiry

Which soil holds more water—potting soil or sandy soil? Write a hypothesis. Then plan and conduct an investigation to find out.

Materials

Here are some materials that you might use.
List additional materials that you need.

- 2 soil samples
- small paper plates
- water

1. Write a hypothesis for this investigation.

   _____

   _____

2. Draw a data table for your investigation in the space below. Record your observations in the table.

3. Did the investigation support your hypothesis? Explain.

   _____

   _____

   _____

LM 102   Lab Manual   (page 3 of 3)   Use with page 331.

Name _____

Date _____

Investigate Log

Pollution and Plants

Materials

- 3 clear plastic cups
- potting soil
- grass seeds
- measuring cup
- clean water
- salt water
- oily water

Procedure

1. Your teacher will provide you with three containers of water. One will have clean water, one will have water polluted with salt, and one will have water polluted with oil.

2. Fill the three plastic cups with potting soil. Plant three seeds in each cup. **Measure** 10 mL of clean water. Water the seeds in the first cup with the clean water, and label the cup. Repeat with the other two cups and containers of water.

3. Place the cups in a sunny window. Every day, water each cup with the water it was first watered with.

4. **Observe** the cups for 10 days. Each day, **record** your observations.

Day	Clean Water	Salty Water	Oily Water
1			
2			
3			
4			
5			
6			
7			
8			
9			
10			

Use with pages 340–341.   (page 1 of 3)   Lab Manual   LM 103

Name _____

Investigate Log

Draw Conclusions

1. What did you **observe**?

   _____

   _____

2. Which plants grew best?

   _____

3. **Inquiry Skill—*Compare*** Scientists **compare** things to see how they are alike and how they are different. How are the plants grown with the three kinds of water alike and different?

   _____

   _____

   _____

   _____

> **Inquiry Skill Tip**
>
> When you **compare** things, think about the characteristics that are important for the investigation. Sometimes you need to consider the way things look. Other times you need to consider the way things behave.

Investigate Self-Assessment	Agree	Not Sure	Disagree
I followed the directions for this investigation.			
I used the graduated cylinder to measure the water.			
I **compared** the growth of the plants.			

LM 104 Lab Manual   (page 2 of 3)   Use with pages 340–341.

Name _____
Date _____

Investigate Log

Independent Inquiry

Would watering plants with water containing vinegar or dish detergent affect their growth? Predict what would happen. Then try it! Make sure to wear goggles.

Materials

Here are some materials that you might use.
List additional materials that you need.

- 3 clear plastic cups
- grass seeds
- potting soil
- graduate
- vinegar
- water
- dish detergent
- safety goggles

1. Write your prediction.

   _____

   _____

2. Use the table below to record your observations.

Week	Clean Water	Vinegar	Dish Detergent
1			
2			
3			
4			

3. Were the results of the investigation the same as your prediction? Explain.

   _____

   _____

Use with page 341.

Name _____

Date _____

Investigate Log

Taking a Look at Trash

Materials

large plastic trash bags

bathroom scale

calculator

Procedure

1. With the rest of your class, save all the paper you would normally throw away for one week.

2. At the end of each day, weigh the paper. **Record** the weight.

3. Use your data to make a line graph showing the weight of each day's collection.

4. Add up all the weights shown on your graph. The sum tells how many pounds of paper the class collected in one week.

Day	Weight of Trash (lb)
1	
2	
3	
4	
5	

Total Weight:

LM 106   Lab Manual   (page 1 of 3)   Use with pages 350–351.

Name _____

Investigate Log

Draw Conclusions

1. Suppose that 1 lb of paper takes up 2 cubic ft of space. How much landfill space would your class save by recycling the paper you saved this week?

   _____

   _____

2. **Inquiry Skill**—*Use Numbers* There are many ways you can communicate an idea. In this investigation, you **used numbers** to describe the weight of the paper collected. How does using numbers help you tell people what you found out?

   _____

   _____

   _____

Inquiry Skill Tip

When you **use numbers** to record data, you should be careful to record the correct numbers. If you record a number wrong, it could make the rest of your data wrong.

Investigate Self-Assessment	Agree	Not Sure	Disagree
I followed the directions for collecting the paper.			
I used the scale to measure the weight of the paper.			
I **communicated** with numbers by making a graph of my measurements.			

Use with pages 350–351.   Lab Manual LM 107

Name _____
Date _____

Investigate Log

Independent Inquiry

Predict how much paper your class could save by using both sides of each sheet. Plan and conduct an investigation to find out.

Materials
Here are some materials that you might use. List additional materials that you need.   • bathroom scale   • calculator

1. Write your prediction.

   _____

2. Draw a table below to record your observations.

3. Calculate how much paper your class could save each week based on the results of your investigation. Explain whether you think the class could actually save this much paper.

   _____

   _____

   _____

Name _____

Date _____

Unit Inquiry Log

Unit D

Space Suits

1. Observe and Ask Questions

Astronauts have to wear special suits during space walks. Moving in a space suit is not easy. What kind of gloves would make it easier for an astronaut to make repairs to the space shuttle in space? Make a list of questions you have about moving around in a space suit. Then circle a question you want to investigate.

_____

2. Form a Hypothesis

Write a hypothesis. A hypothesis is a suggested answer to the question you are testing.

_____

3. Plan an Experiment

Identify and Control Variables

To plan your experiment, you must first identify the important variables. Complete the statements below.

The variable I will change is

_____.

The variables I will observe or measure are

_____.

The variables I will keep the same, or *control*, are

_____.

Use with page 363.

Name _____

Unit Inquiry Log

Develop a Procedure and Gather Materials Write the steps you will follow to set up an experiment and collect data.

_____
_____
_____
_____
_____
_____
_____

Use extra sheets of blank paper if you need to write down more steps.

Materials List Look carefully at all the steps of your procedure, and list all the materials you will use. Be sure that your teacher approves your plan and your materials list before you begin.

_____
_____
_____
_____
_____
_____
_____

Name _____

Unit Inquiry Log

4. Conduct the Experiment

Gather and Record Data Follow your plan and collect data. Use the table below or a table you design to record your data. **Observe** carefully. **Record** your observations and be sure to note anything unusual or unexpected.

Description of Gloves	Thickness of Gloves (cm)	Time Needed to Tighten Bolt

Use with page 363.   (page 3 of 4)   Lab Manual   LM 111

Name _____

Unit Inquiry Log

Interpret Data Make a graph of the data you have collected. Plot the data on a sheet of graph paper or use a software program.

5. **Draw Conclusions and Communicate Results**

   Compare the **hypothesis** with the data and the graphs. Then answer these questions.

   1. Given the results of the experiment, do you think the hypothesis was correct? Explain.

      _____

      _____

   2. How would you revise the hypothesis? Explain.

      _____

      _____

   3. What else did you observe during the experiment?

      _____

      _____

Prepare a presentation for your classmates to **communicate** what you have learned. Display your data tables and graphs.

Investigate Further

Write another hypothesis that you might investigate.

_____

_____

LM 112   Lab Manual   (page 4 of 4)   Use with page 363.

Name _____
Date _____

Investigate Log

Where in the World Is Water?

Materials

plastic inflatable globe

blank sheet of paper

pencil

Procedure

1. Work in a group of five. Choose one person to be the recorder.
2. The other four persons toss the globe gently to one another.
3. The catcher catches the globe with open hands. The recorder **records the data** of whether the catcher's right index finger touches land or touches water.
4. Continue tossing and recording until the globe has been tossed 20 times.

Location	Number of Catches	Total
Land		
Water		

Use with pages 368–369.

Name _____

Investigate Log

Draw Conclusions

1. Total the catches. How many times did the catcher's right index finger touch water? How many times did it touch land?

   _____
   _____
   _____

2. Where did the catcher's finger land more often? Why do you think this happened?

   _____
   _____

3. **Inquiry Skill—*Collect Data*** Scientists **use numbers** to **collect data**. Using your data, estimate how much of Earth's surface is covered by water.

   _____
   _____

> **Inquiry Skill Tip**
>
> You often use a measuring tool, such as a ruler or a thermometer, when you **collect data**. In this Investigate, you collect data by putting tally marks in the correct spaces of a data table. Making good observations is an important part of collecting data.

Investigate Self-Assessment	Agree	Not Sure	Disagree
I followed the directions for this investigation.			
I worked well with others in my group.			
I was able to **collect data** and use it for my estimate.			

Name _____
Date _____

Investigate Log

Independent Inquiry

The more data you collect, the more accurate your data will be. How would doing the Investigate 10 more times change your data? Try it! Communicate your results in a bar graph.

Materials

Here are some materials that you might use. List additional materials that you need.

- plastic inflatable globe
- graph paper
- pencil

1. Predict how many times the catcher's finger will touch water and how many times it will touch land.

   _____
   _____

2. Record and total the catches on the data table below. Make a bar graph.

Location	Number of Catches	Independent Inquiry Total
Land		
Water		

3. Explain how doing the investigation 10 more times changed your results.

   _____
   _____

Use with page 369. (page 3 of 3) Lab Manual LM 115

Name _____

Date _____

Investigate Log

Condensation in a Terrarium

Materials

clear plastic salad container   soil   packet of seeds   water   spray bottle

Procedure

1. To build a terrarium, put about 3 cm of soil in a clear plastic salad container.

2. Plant the seeds. Follow the instructions on the seed package.

3. Using a spray bottle, spray the soil until it is moist. Close the lid of the container, and label the container with your name.

4. Place the terrarium next to a sunny window or under a lamp. **Observe** your terrarium for several days. Write down all the changes you see.

Day	Observations

Name _____

Investigate Log

Draw Conclusions

1. What changes happened inside the terrarium?

   _____

   _____

2. Did anything in the terrarium remind you of weather? If so, what was it?

   _____

   _____

3. **Inquiry Skill—***Infer* You watered your terrarium only one time. **Infer** how water may have gotten on the lid of the terrarium.

   _____

   _____

Inquiry Skill Tip

A good way to find possible answers in science is to **infer**. Think about the facts you already know. Then think about your observations. Use what you already know to explain what you have observed.

Investigate Self-Assessment	Agree	Not Sure	Disagree
I made observations that helped me with this investigation.			
I washed my hands after handling the soil and seeds.			
I was able to **infer** how water got on the lid of the terrarium.			

Use with pages 378–379.   (page 2 of 3)   Lab Manual LM 117

Name _____
Date _____

Investigate Log

Independent Inquiry

Do the same Investigate, but don't close the lid. What do you think will happen? Compare your observations with the lid closed and not closed.

Materials

Here are some materials that you might use.
List additional materials that you need.

- soil
- packet of seeds
- water
- spray bottle
- clear plastic salad container

1. Predict how your observations will change when the lid of the terrarium is not closed.

   _____

2. Observe your terrarium for several days. Write down all the changes you see.

Day	Observations

3. Compare your observations of the terrarium with the lid closed and with the lid not closed. Explain any differences.

   _____

   _____

Name _____

Date _____

Investigate Log

Measuring Wind

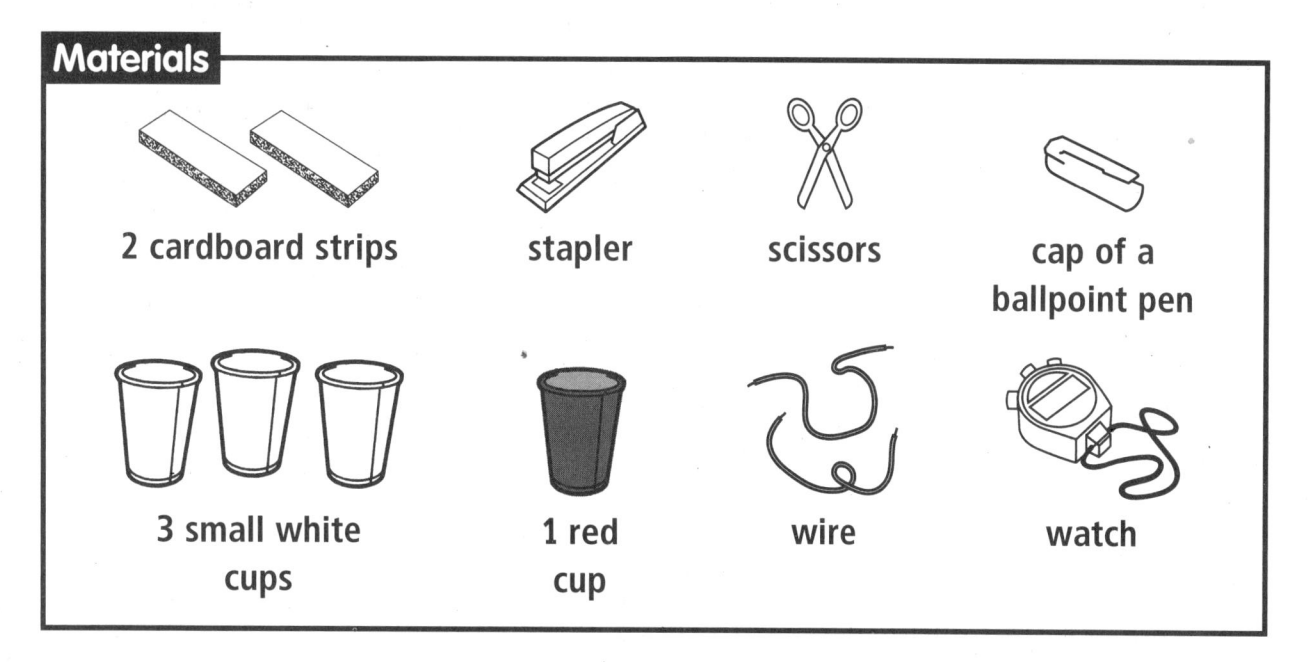

Materials

- 2 cardboard strips
- stapler
- scissors
- cap of a ballpoint pen
- 3 small white cups
- 1 red cup
- wire
- watch

Procedure

1. Make an X with the cardboard strips. Staple them together.

2. **CAUTION: Carefully use scissors to make a hole in the middle of the X. Push the pen cap into the hole.**

3. Cut a slit in both sides of each cup. Attach a cup to the end of each cardboard strip by pushing the cardboard through the slits.

4. Push most of the wire into the ground. Balance the pen cap on the wire.

5. **Observe** the cups for one minute. Count the number of times the red cup spins by. **Record** your data.

6. Repeat your observation at the same time each day for a week.

Day	Number of Turns
1	
2	
3	
4	
5	
6	
7	

Use with pages 388–389.

Name _____

Investigate Log

Draw Conclusions

1. Make a bar graph that shows the number of turns the cup made on each day of the week.

Inquiry Skill Tip

When you want to **compare** data, putting it in a bar graph can help. A bar graph shows all the data side by side.

2. Inquiry Skill—*Compare* How did making a graph help **compare** your results?

_____

_____

_____

_____

Investigate Self-Assessment	Agree	Not Sure	Disagree
I followed the directions for this investigation.			
I was careful when I used scissors.			
I was able to **compare** my results with a bar graph.			

LM 120 Lab Manual

Name _____
Date _____

Investigate Log

Independent Inquiry

Predict what would happen if you added 2 more cups. Try it.

Materials

Here are some materials that you might use.
List additional materials that you need.

- 3 cardboard strips
- cap of a ballpoint pen
- wire
- stapler
- 5 small white paper cups
- watch
- scissors
- 1 red paper cup

1. Predict whether the cups will move faster, slower, or stay the same.

   _____
   _____
   _____

2. Draw a data table below. Record the number of times the red cup spins by.

3. Compare the results of this investigation with your prediction. Was your prediction correct?

   _____
   _____

Use with page 389.   (page 3 of 3)   Lab Manual LM 121

Name _____
Date _____

Investigate Log

How Sunlight Strikes Earth

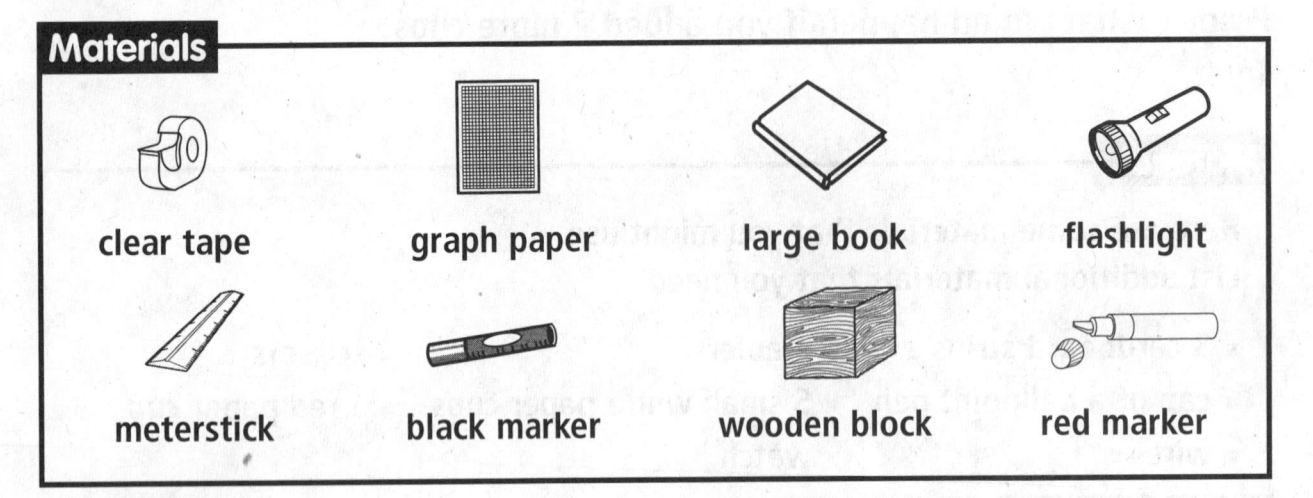

Materials

- clear tape
- graph paper
- large book
- flashlight
- meterstick
- black marker
- wooden block
- red marker

Procedure

1. Tape graph paper to a book. Hold a flashlight about 50 cm above the paper. Shine the light straight down. You will see a circle of light on the paper.

2. Have a partner use the black marker to trace the circle of light. **Observe** the light on the paper. **Record** the number of squares inside the black line.

3. Keep the flashlight in the same position. Have a partner put the block under one end of the book. This time, use the red marker to trace the light on the paper. **Observe** the light on the paper, and **record** the number of squares inside the red line.

Light Beam	Brightness	Number of Squares
Straight		
Tilted		

LM 122 Lab Manual   (page 1 of 3)   Use with pages 406–407.

Name _____

Investigate Log

Draw Conclusions

1. Inside which line was the light brighter? Inside which line are there more squares?

   _____

2. **Inquiry Skill—*Compare*** Compare the ways the light rays struck the straight and tilted surfaces. At which time would you infer that a place on Earth has warmer weather—when the sun's rays strike it directly or when they strike it at a slant? Explain.

   _____

   _____

   _____

Inquiry Skill Tip

When you **compare** things in an investigation, think about the properties you are studying. For this Investigate, you are interested in the direction at which the light struck the surface.

Investigate Self-Assessment	Agree	Not Sure	Disagree
I followed the directions for this investigation.			
I used the ruler to measure the distance from the flashlight to the book.			
I was able to **compare** the ways the light rays struck the straight and tilted surfaces.			

Use with pages 406–407. Lab Manual

Name _____

Date _____

Investigate Log

Independent Inquiry

Form a hypothesis about what will happen if the book is tilted even more. Plan and conduct an experiment to test your idea.

Materials

Here are some materials that you might use.
List additional materials that you need.

- clear tape
- large book
- meterstick
- wooden block
- graph paper
- flashlight
- black marker

1. Write your hypothesis.

   _____

   _____

2. Record your observations on the data table below.

Light Beam	Brightness	Number of Squares
Tilted More		

3. What can you conclude from your investigation?

   _____

   _____

LM 124 Lab Manual   Use with page 407.

Name _____

Date _____

Investigate Log

The Moon's Phases

Materials

flashlight   volleyball

Procedure

1 Work in groups of three. Use the picture in Step 1 in your textbook to set up the area. Your teacher will darken the room. One classmate will hold a volleyball at position 1. Another classmate will shine a flashlight on it. The third group member will stand in the middle and **observe** the ball and make a drawing of the ball's lighted side.

2 The classmate holding the volleyball will move to positions 2, 3, and 4. Keep rotating to face the classmate with the volleyball. **Observe** and **record** the light at each position.

3 Switch roles so that everyone can **observe** the pattern.

Position 1	Position 2
Position 3	Position 4

Use with pages 416–417.   (page 1 of 3)   Lab Manual   **LM 125**

Name _____

Investigate Log

Draw Conclusions

1. What part of the ball was lighted at each position?

   _____

2. What does the ball represent? The flashlight? The person recording?

   _____

   _____

3. **Inquiry Skill—*Infer*** If the ball represents the moon, what can you **infer** that the different parts of the lighted ball represent?

   _____

> **Inquiry Skill Tip**
>
> When you **infer**, you use your observations and what you already know to figure something out.

Investigate Self-Assessment	Agree	Not Sure	Disagree
I followed the directions for this investigation.			
I worked with a group to make observations.			
I was able to **infer** what the different parts of the lighted ball represent.			

Name _____

Date _____

Investigate Log

Independent Inquiry

The moon's phases occur in a regular pattern. Predict how long it will take the moon to go through all its phases. Test your prediction.

Materials

Here are some materials that you might use.
List additional materials that you need.

- paper
- pencil

1. Write your prediction for this investigation.

   _____

   _____

2. Describe your investigation and your predictions.

   _____

   _____

   _____

   _____

3. Explain how the outcome of your investigation is the same as or different from your prediction.

   _____

   _____

Use with page 417.   Lab Manual LM 127

Name _____
Date _____

Investigate Log

The Planets

Materials

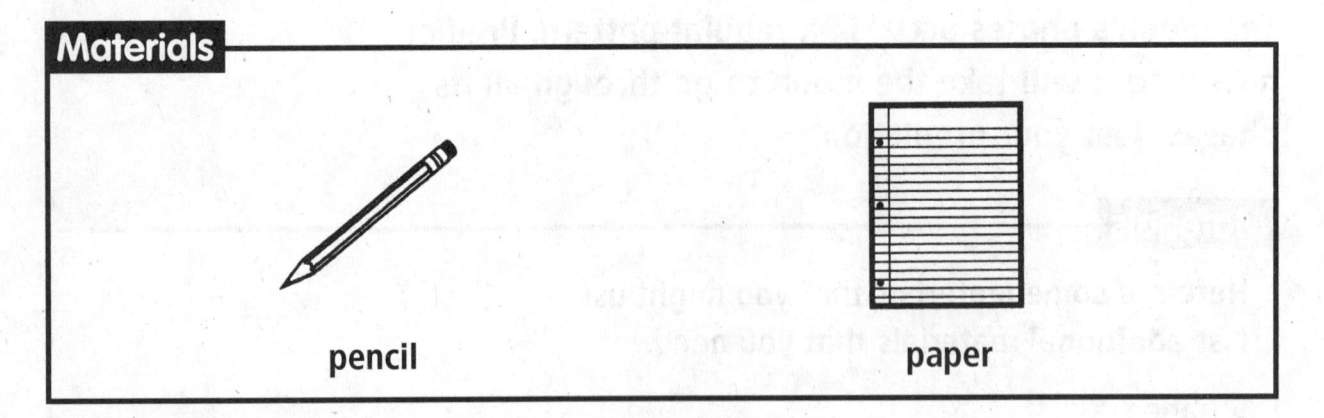

pencil   paper

Procedure

1. **Use numbers** from the Planet Data table in your textbook to list the planets in **order** by their distance from the sun, from closest to farthest.

2. Next to the planets' names, **record** their distances from the sun.

Order of Planets and "Dwarf Planets"	Distance from the Sun (in millions of kilometers)

LM 128   Lab Manual   (page 1 of 3)   Use with pages 426–427.

Name _____

Investigate Log

Draw Conclusions

1. Which planet is closest to the sun?
   _____

2. Which planet is farthest from the sun?
   _____

3. How many planets are between Earth and the sun?
   _____

4. Which planets are Earth's nearest neighbors?
   _____

5. **Inquiry Skill—*Use Numbers*** Scientists sometimes **use numbers** to put things in order. List other ways you could order the planets.

   _____

Inquiry Skill Tip

You often need to compare when you **use numbers** in an investigation. First, notice how many digits the numbers have. A number with fewer digits is lower than a number with more digits. If the number of digits is the same, start with the digits on the left when you compare.

Investigate Self-Assessment	Agree	Not Sure	Disagree
I listed the planets in order by their distance from the sun.			
I recorded the distances of the planets from the sun.			
I was able to **use numbers** to order the planets from the closest to the farthest.			

Use with pages 426–427.

Name _____
Date _____

Investigate Log

Independent Inquiry

How could you use numbers to help you plan a model of the solar system? Plan a simple investigation for the model.

Materials
Here are some materials that you might use. List additional materials that you need. • pencil • paper

1. What numbers do you need to use to help you plan your model?

   _____

   _____

2. Write a plan for your model.

   _____

   _____

   _____

3. How will your model help you learn about the solar system?

   _____

   _____

   _____

LM 130 Lab Manual   Use with page 427.

Name _____

Date _____

Unit Inquiry Log

Unit E

Mold Sand

1. Observe and Ask Questions

Building a large sand sculpture is not always easy. What can you add to sand to make it easier to build a sand sculpture? Make a list of questions you have about the sand in a good sand sculpture. Then circle a question you want to investigate.

_____

2. Form a Hypothesis

Write a hypothesis. A hypothesis is a suggested answer to the question you are testing.

_____

3. Plan an Experiment

Identify and Control Variables

To plan your experiment, you must first identify the important variables. Complete the statements below.

The variable I will change is

_____.

The variables I will observe or measure are

_____.

The variables I will keep the same, or *control*, are

_____.

Use with page 451.　　　(page 1 of 4)　　　Lab Manual　LM 131

Name _____

Unit Inquiry Log

Develop a Procedure and Gather Materials Write the steps you will follow to set up an experiment and collect data.

_____
_____
_____
_____
_____
_____
_____

Use extra sheets of blank paper if you need to write down more steps.

Materials List Look carefully at all the steps of your procedure, and list all the materials you will use. Be sure that your teacher approves your plan and your materials list before you begin.

_____
_____
_____
_____
_____
_____
_____

Name _____

Unit Inquiry Log

4. Conduct the Experiment

Gather and Record Data Follow your plan and collect data. Use the table below or a table you design to record your data. **Observe** carefully. **Record** your observations and be sure to note anything unusual or unexpected.

Amount of sand in each sculpture: _____ g

Sand pile number	Amount of water added to sand pile (mL)	Amount of sand that fell off of sand sculpture (g)
1		
2		
3		
4		
5		
6		
7		
8		

Use with page 451.

Name _____

Unit Inquiry Log

Interpret Data Make a graph of the data you have collected. Plot the data on a sheet of graph paper or use a software program.

5. **Draw Conclusions and Communicate Results**

   Compare the hypothesis with the data and the graphs. Then answer these questions.

   1. Given the results of the experiment, do you think the hypothesis was correct? Explain.

      _____
      _____

   2. How would you revise the hypothesis? Explain.

      _____
      _____

   3. What else did you observe during the experiment?

      _____
      _____

Prepare a presentation for your classmates to communicate what you have learned. Display your data tables and graphs.

Investigate Further

Write another hypothesis that you might investigate.

_____
_____

LM 134 Lab Manual

Name _____

Date _____

Investigate Log

Measuring Volume

Materials

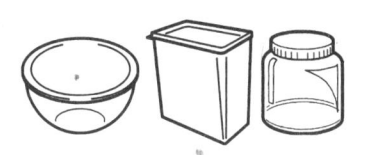

metric measuring cup | water | 3 clear containers of different shapes | masking tape

Procedure

1. In a metric measuring cup, **measure** 100 mL of water.

2. Pour the water into a clear container.

3. Use a piece of masking tape to mark the level of the water in the container. Put the bottom edge of the tape at the water line.

4. Repeat Steps 1–3 until all three containers have 100 mL of water in them, and all three levels are marked.

Container #1	Container #2	Container #3

Use with pages 456–457.   (page 1 of 3)   Lab Manual   LM 135

Name _____

Investigate Log

Draw Conclusions

Inquiry Skill Tip

Use data, observations, and facts you have learned to **predict** what you think will happen in the future.

1. How much water is in each container?

   _____

2. Describe the height of the water in each container. Explain why the height of the water looks different in each container.

   _____

   _____

3. **Inquiry Skill—*Predict*** Scientists use data and observations to **predict** what will happen. What do you **predict** will happen if you pour the water from each container back into the measuring cup?

   _____

   _____

Investigate Self-Assessment	Agree	Not Sure	Disagree
I followed the directions for this investigation.			
I used the measuring cup to measure 100 mL of water for each container.			
I **predicted** what would happen if I poured the water from each container back into the measuring cup.			

LM 136 Lab Manual   (page 2 of 3)   Use with pages 456–457.

Name _____

Date _____

Investigate Log

Independent Inquiry

Fill three different-shaped containers with water. Predict how much water is in each container. Measure the water in each container. How close were your predictions?

Materials

Here are some materials that you might use.
List additional materials that you need.

- metric measuring cup
- 3 clear containers of different shapes
- water
- masking tape

1. Fill each container with water. Use the table below to record your prediction for the volume of water in each container.

Container	Predicted Volume (ml)
1	
2	
3	

2. Measure the water in each container. Record the volumes in the table below.

Container	Measured Volume (ml)
1	
2	
3	

3. What can you conclude about the relationship between the volume of water, the level of the water, and the shape of the container?

_____

_____

Use with page 457.

Name _____

Date _____

Investigate Log

Temperature and Matter

Materials

- metric measuring cup
- hot water
- plastic jar or beaker
- thermometer
- 3 ice cubes
- plastic spoon

Procedure

1. **Measure** 200 mL of hot water from the tap in the measuring cup. Pour the water into a jar or beaker.
2. **Measure** the temperature of the water with a thermometer. **Record** the data.
3. Add an ice cube to the water. Stir with a plastic spoon. **Record** what you **observe.**
4. **Measure** the temperature of the water again. **Record** the data.
5. Repeat Steps 3 and 4 twice.

Step	Observations	Temperature (°C)
Hot water		
After 1 ice cube		
After 2 ice cubes		
After 3 ice cubes		

LM 138   Lab Manual   (page 1 of 3)   Use with pages 468–469.

Name _____

Investigate Log

Draw Conclusions

1. What happened to the ice cubes in the water?

   _____

2. What happened to the temperature of the water each time you added an ice cube?

   _____

3. **Inquiry Skill—*Communicate*** One way scientists can **communicate** data is in a bar graph. Make a bar graph to **communicate** what happened to the temperature of the water in this activity.

> **Inquiry Skill Tip**
>
> You can use tables, charts, drawings, line graphs, or circle graphs to **communicate** what happened in an investigation. When deciding which method to use, consider the message that you want to communicate. For example, in this Investigate, you use a bar graph because you need to compare temperatures for different numbers of ice cubes.

Investigate Self-Assessment	Agree	Not Sure	Disagree
I followed the directions for this investigation.			
I used the thermometer to measure the temperature of the water.			
I **communicated** my data by making a bar graph.			

Use with pages 468–469.

Name _____

Date _____

Investigate Log

Independent Inquiry

Put 100 mL of water in a freezer. Take it out every 10 minutes and measure its temperature. Communicate the data in a bar graph. Interpret the data.

Materials

Here are some materials that you might use.
List additional materials that you need.

- metric measuring cup
- plastic jar or beaker
- water
- freezer
- thermometer
- timer or clock

1. What will this investigation test?

   _____

2. Record your measurements in the data table below. Make a bar graph to communicate the results.

Time (min)	Temperature (°C)
0	
10	
20	
30	
40	
50	
60	

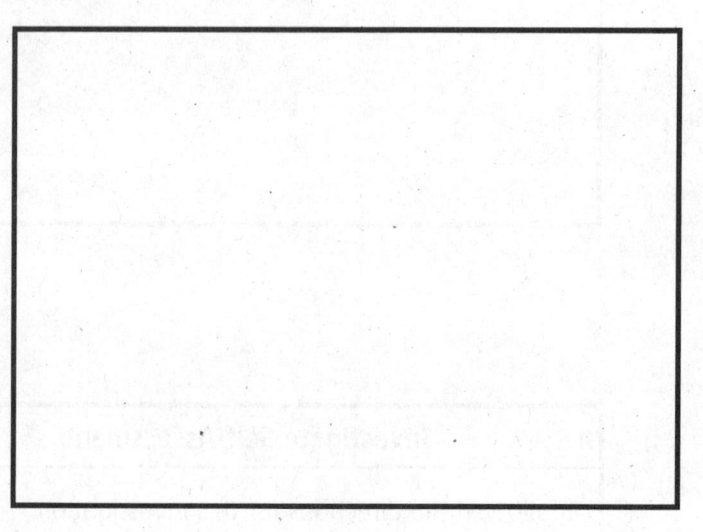

3. Interpret the data in the graph. What can you conclude about the temperatures of the water and the freezer?

   _____

   _____

LM 140 Lab Manual   (page 3 of 3)   Use with page 469.

Name _____

Date _____

Investigate Log

Will It Mix?

Materials

- metric measuring cup
- 2 clear plastic jars
- measuring spoon ($\frac{1}{4}$ teaspoon)
- plastic spoon
- sand
- water
- hand lens
- salt

Procedure

1. **Measure** 200 mL of water. Pour the water into a jar.

2. Add $\frac{1}{4}$ teaspoon of sand to the water and stir. Use a hand lens to **observe** the jar's contents. **Record** what you **observe**.

3. Repeat Step 1, using the other jar.

4. Add $\frac{1}{4}$ teaspoon of salt to the water and stir. Use a hand lens to **observe** the jar's contents. **Record** what you **observe**.

5. Repeat Step 4 until you see salt collect on the bottom of the jar after you stir. **Record** the number of teaspoons used in all.

Material	Observations
Sand	
Salt	Total number of teaspoonfuls used: _____

Use with pages 478–479.   (page 1 of 3)   Lab Manual   LM 141

Name _____

Investigate Log

Draw Conclusions

1. What did you **observe** when you stirred in the sand? The salt?

   _____

2. **Inquiry Skill**—*Communicate* Scientists sometimes use drawings to **communicate**. Make two drawings that will **communicate** what happened to the sand and the salt when they were stirred into the water.

> **Inquiry Skill Tip**
>
> If you use drawings to **communicate**, make the drawings clear and simple. Be sure they show the details you want to communicate. If necessary, use labels to explain the drawings.

Sand	Salt

Investigate Self-Assessment	Agree	Not Sure	Disagree
I observed what happened when I mixed sand into water and salt into water.			
I used the measuring spoon to measure the amount of salt I added to the water.			
I **communicated** my observations by making drawings.			

LM 142 Lab Manual   (page 2 of 3)   Use with pages 478–479.

Name _____
Date _____

Investigate Log

Independent Inquiry

What do you predict will happen if you leave the jar of salt water in a warm place? Try it. Was your prediction correct?

Materials

Here are some materials that you might use.
List additional materials that you need.

- jar with salt water

1. What do you think will happen if you leave the jar with salt water in a warm place?

   _____

   _____

2. Leave the jar in a warm place for a week. Make a drawing to communicate the results.

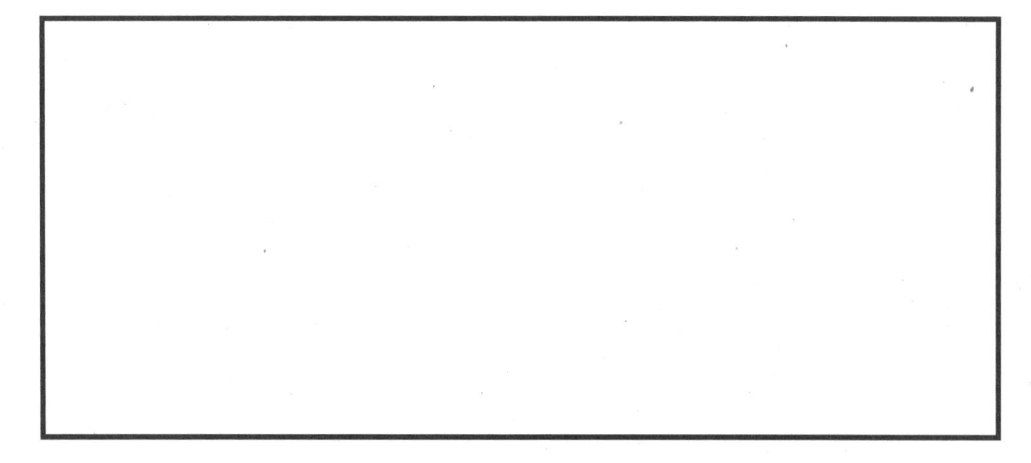

3. Did the results agree with your prediction? Explain.

   _____

   _____

Use with page 479.   Lab Manual   LM 143

Name _____
Date _____

Investigate Log

Observing Temperature

Materials

thermometer   clock

Procedure

1. With your group, find a place outside that is sunny all day long.

2. In the morning, have a group member place the thermometer on the ground face up.

3. Wait a few minutes until the temperature reading stops changing.

4. Each member of the group should read and **record** the temperature.

5. **Observe** the thermometer once an hour for several hours. **Communicate** your observations in a line graph that shows time and temperature.

Time (hr)	Temperature (°C)
0	
1	
2	
3	

LM 144   Lab Manual   (page 1 of 3)   Use with pages 494–495.

Name _____

Investigate Log

Draw Conclusions

1. What changes did you **observe**? What caused these changes?

   _____

   _____

2. **Inquiry Skill—*Infer*** Scientists use their observations to **infer** why things happen. The rising temperature on the thermometer was caused by energy. Where can you **infer** the energy came from?

   _____

Inquiry Skill Tip

To **infer** why something happened, make a list of all the things that changed in your investigation. Decide which of these was a "cause" and which was an "effect."

Investigate Self-Assessment	Agree	Not Sure	Disagree
I followed the directions for this investigation.			
I used the thermometer to measure the temperature several times.			
I **inferred** where the energy that caused the temperature increase came from.			

Use with pages 494–495.   (page 2 of 3)   Lab Manual   **LM 145**

Name _____

Date _____

Investigate Log

Independent Inquiry

Do you think you would see similar changes on a cloudy day? Make a hypothesis. Then plan and conduct a simple investigation to test it.

Materials

Here are some materials that you might use.
List additional materials that you need.

- thermometer
- clock

1. Write your hypothesis for this investigation.

   _____

   _____

   _____

   _____

2. Use the table below to record your temperature measurements.

Time (hr)	Temperature (°C)
0	
1	
2	
3	

3. What conclusions can you draw from your investigation and data?

   _____

   _____

   _____

Name _____

Date _____

Investigate Log

The Heat Is On

Materials

clear plastic cup   thermometer   ice cubes

Procedure

1. Fill a clear plastic cup with ice cubes. Place a thermometer in the cup. Place the cup in sunlight.

2. After several minutes, **record** the temperature inside the cup. Use the table below.

3. Continue to **record** the temperature inside the cup every half hour for three hours.

4. **Communicate** the data from your table by making a bar graph.

Time (hr)	Temperature (°C)
0	
$\frac{1}{2}$	
1	
$1\frac{1}{2}$	
2	
$2\frac{1}{2}$	
3	

Use with pages 504–505.

Name _____

Investigate Log

Draw Conclusions

1. What did you **observe** about the temperature and the ice? What caused these changes?

   _____
   _____
   _____

2. **Inquiry Skill—*Infer*** Scientists use observations and data to **infer** why things happen. What can you **infer** happens to an object placed in sunlight?

   _____
   _____

> **Inquiry Skill Tip**
>
> You may observe many changes during an investigation. To **infer** why things happen, notice whether the measurements you make have increased or decreased at different times. A change in temperature means that energy has moved from one place to another. Think about what would cause this movement of energy.

Investigate Self-Assessment	Agree	Not Sure	Disagree
I followed the directions for this investigation.			
I used the thermometer to measure the temperature inside the cup.			
I **inferred** what happens to an object placed in sunlight.			

LM 148   Lab Manual   (page 2 of 3)   Use with pages 504–505.

Name _____
Date _____

Investigate Log

Independent Inquiry

What do you think happens to the temperature of water placed in a freezer? Make a hypothesis. Then test it.

Materials

Here are some materials that you might use.
List additional materials that you need.

- clear plastic cup
- thermometer
- freezer
- water

1. Write your hypothesis for this investigation.

_____

_____

2. Use the table below to record your observations.

Time (hr)	Temperature (°C)
0	
$\frac{1}{2}$	
1	
$1\frac{1}{2}$	
2	
$2\frac{1}{2}$	
3	

3. Did your observations support your hypothesis? Explain.

_____

_____

Use with page 505. (page 3 of 3) Lab Manual LM 149

Name _____

Date _____

Investigate Log

Make a Paper Windmill

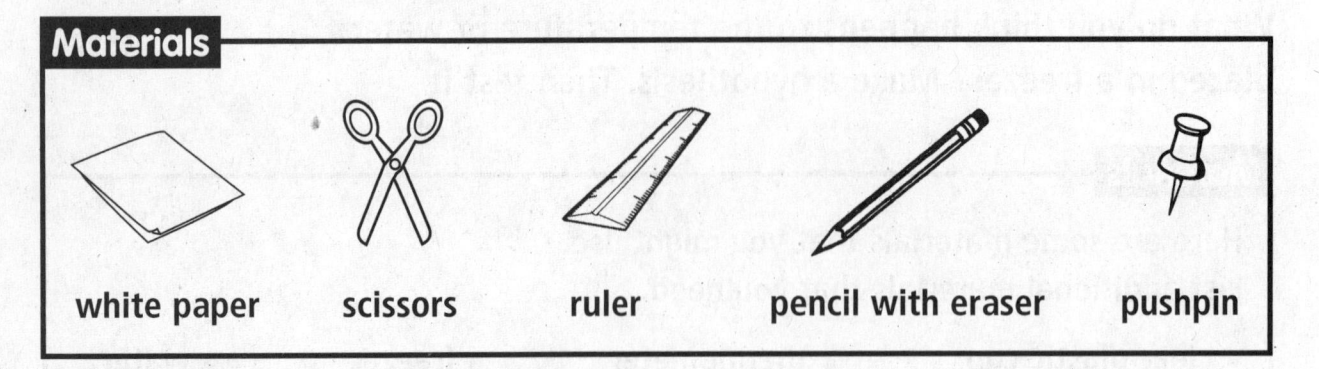

Materials

white paper   scissors   ruler   pencil with eraser   pushpin

Procedure

1. Draw a 12 cm square with dotted lines and dots as shown in your textbook.
2. Use scissors to cut out the square.
3. Cut along each of the dotted lines to within 1 cm of the center.
4. One at a time, take each corner with a dot, and fold it toward the center of the square to make a vane.
5. **CAUTION: Pushpins are sharp!** Put the pushpin through the center of all the folded corners and into the eraser of the pencil. Be sure the vanes turn freely.
6. You have just **made a model** of a windmill. First, blow gently on the windmill. Then blow more forcefully. Record what you observed each time.

Action	Observation
While blowing gently	
While blowing forcefully	

LM 150   Lab Manual   (page 1 of 3)   Use with pages 512–513.

Name _____

Investigate Log

Draw Conclusions

1. What did you **observe** when you blew on the windmill each time?

   _____
   _____

2. **Inquiry Skill—***Use Models* Scientists **use models** to help them understand processes. How does a windmill work? What kind of energy turns a windmill?

Inquiry Skill Tip

When you **use a model** to understand processes, think about which parts of the model move or change in some way. Consider what causes the movement or the change.

_____
_____
_____
_____

Investigate Self-Assessment	Agree	Not Sure	Disagree
I followed the directions for making a paper windmill.			
I was careful when I used the sharp pushpins.			
I **used a model** to determine how a windmill works.			

Use with pages 512–513. (page 2 of 3) Lab Manual LM 151

Name _____

Date _____

Investigate Log

Independent Inquiry

Fold each corner with a dot backward instead of forward. What do you predict will happen to your windmill in a breeze? Try it.

Materials

Here are some materials that you might use.
List additional materials that you need.

- white paper
- scissors
- ruler
- pushpin
- pencil with eraser

1. Write your prediction for the investigation.

   _____

   _____

2. Observe how the windmill moves after you fold the edges of each corner backward. Record your observations below.

   _____

   _____

   _____

3. Did the outcome of your investigation agree with your prediction? Explain.

   _____

   _____

   _____

LM 152 Lab Manual — Use with page 513.

Name _____

Date _____

Investigate Log

Looking for Static Electricity

Materials

tissue paper   comb   piece of wool (sweater or blanket)

Procedure

1. Tear a small piece of tissue paper into tiny bits. Make the pieces smaller than your fingertips. Put the pieces in a pile.

2. Hold the comb just above the pile. What happens? **Record** what you **observe**.

3. Pass the comb through your hair several times. Repeat Step 2.

4. Rub the comb with your hand. Repeat Step 2.

5. Rub the comb with a piece of wool. Repeat Step 2.

Action	Observations
Comb not passed through hair or rubbed with wool	
Comb passed through hair	
Comb rubbed with wool	

Use with pages 526–527.   (page 1 of 3)   Lab Manual   LM 153

Name _____

Investigate Log

Draw Conclusions

1. How did the comb change after you passed it through your hair? What happened when you rubbed the comb with wool?

   _____
   _____
   _____

2. **Inquiry Skill—*Hypothesize*** When you **hypothesize**, you use observations or data to give a reason something happens. State a hypothesis to explain what happened in this investigation.

   _____
   _____
   _____

Inquiry Skill Tip

A **hypothesis** is sometimes called an "educated guess." You should base your ideas on things you observe and things you already know. By combining these, you can decide what is probably the reason something happens. Your hypothesis may not be supported by data. It still can guide you in investigating your ideas.

Investigate Self-Assessment	Agree	Not Sure	Disagree
I followed the directions for this investigation.			
I **observed** what happened to the bits of tissue paper.			
I **hypothesized** what happened in this investigation.			

LM 154 Lab Manual   Use with pages 526–527.

Name _____

Date _____

Investigate Log

Independent Inquiry

Do you get the same result if you rub the comb with other things, such as silk or plastic wrap? Plan and conduct an experiment to find out.

Materials

Here are some materials that you might use.
List additional materials that you need.

- tissue paper
- comb

1. Predict whether the comb will attract the bits of tissue paper after being rubbed with each of the objects.

_____

_____

_____

2. Use the table below to record your observations.

Object	Observations

3. Were your predictions correct? Explain.

_____

_____

Use with page 527. Lab Manual LM 155

Name _____

Date _____

Investigate Log

Which Magnet Is Stronger?

Materials

bar magnet   horseshoe magnet   10 to 20 steel paper clips

Procedure

1. Hold the bar magnet near a paper clip. **Record** what happens.

2. Hold the horseshoe magnet near a paper clip. **Record** what happens.

3. Pick up as many paper clips as one end of the bar magnet will hold. Count them. **Record the data.**

4. Pick up as many paper clips as one end of the horseshoe magnet will hold. Count them. **Record the data.**

Kind of Magnet	Observations	Number of Paper Clips
Bar		
Horseshoe		

LM 156   Lab Manual   (page 1 of 3)   Use with pages 534–535.

Name _____

Investigate Log

Draw Conclusions

1. Which magnet is stronger? How can you tell?

   _____

   _____

2. **Inquiry Skill—*Communicate*** Scientists can **communicate** data in graphs. Make a bar graph to show how many paper clips each magnet held.

Inquiry Skill Tip

Graphs are a good way to **communicate** the data you collect during an investigation. Choose the graph style that best shows the type of data you collect. A bar graph is useful if you want to compare data. A circle graph can be used to show parts of a whole. Line graphs are a good way to communicate changes over time.

Investigate Self-Assessment	Agree	Not Sure	Disagree
I followed the directions for this investigation.			
I was careful not to drop or hit the magnets.			
I was able to **communicate** data in a graph.			

Use with pages 534–535. (page 2 of 3) Lab Manual LM 157

Name _____
Date _____

Investigate Log

Independent Inquiry

If you hold two magnets together, can they lift as many paper clips as each one can separately? Plan an investigation to find out.

Materials

Here are some materials that you might use.
List additional materials that you need.

- 2 bar magnets
- 10 to 20 steel paper clips

1. What will you learn in your investigation?

   _____
   _____

2. Record your observations in the table below.

Number of Magnets	Number of Paper Clips
1	
2	

3. What conclusions can you draw from the results of your investigation? Explain.

   _____
   _____
   _____
   _____

LM 158 Lab Manual   Use with page 535.

Name _____

Date _____

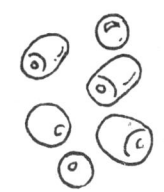

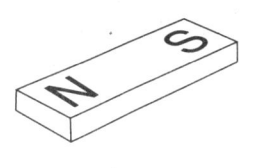

Investigate Log

Simple Sorting

Materials

steel paper clips · bowl or paper plate · plastic beads · magnet · stopwatch

Procedure

1. Put a handful of paper clips in the bowl. Add a handful of beads. Mix them up.

2. Remove the paper clips from the bowl by hand, making sure not to pick up any of the beads. Use a stopwatch to **measure** and **record** how long this takes.

3. Return the paper clips to the bowl of beads. Mix them up again.

4. Now use a magnet to remove the paper clips from the bowl. Use a stopwatch to **measure** and **record** how long this takes.

Method	Time (s)
Without a magnet	
With a magnet	

Use with pages 542–543. (page 1 of 3) Lab Manual LM 159

Name _____

Investigate Log

Draw Conclusions

1. How do the two times **compare**? Which is the quicker way to separate the steel paper clips from the plastic beads?

   _____

   _____

   _____

2. **Inquiry Skill—*Infer*** Scientists use what they know to **infer**, or conclude. Look at the picture on the first page of this lesson in your textbook. What are some things that you can **infer** about the use of an electromagnet?

   _____

   _____

   _____

Inquiry Skill Tip

Good observations are important when you **infer** information. Some of the most important things you learn from an investigation are not specifically found in the results. You have to think about what the results mean.

Investigate Self-Assessment	Agree	Not Sure	Disagree
I followed the directions for separating the paper clips and the beads.			
I used the stopwatch to measure the times needed to separate the objects.			
I was able to **infer** some things about the use of the electromagnet.			

LM 160   Lab Manual   (page 2 of 3)   Use with pages 542–543.

Name _____

Date _____

Investigate Log

Independent Inquiry

Mix various small metal objects together. Predict which objects you can separate by using a magnet. Test your prediction.

Materials

Here are some materials that you might use.
List additional materials that you need.

- steel paper clips
- magnet
- bowl

1. Write your predictions.

   _____

   _____

2. Record which objects were attracted to the magnet and which were not.

Objects attracted to the magnet	Objects not attracted to the magnet

3. Explain how the outcome of this investigation was the same as or different from your predictions.

   _____

   _____

   _____

Use with page 543.   (page 3 of 3)   Lab Manual   LM 161

Name _____

Date _____

Investigate Log

Getting Warmer?

Materials

- safety goggles
- 3 spoons: wooden, plastic, and metal
- hot water
- 3 plastic foam cups
- 3 mugs with handles: ceramic, plastic, and metal

Procedure

1. **CAUTION: Put on safety goggles.**
2. Touch the three spoons. **Record** your **observations**.
3. **CAUTION: Be careful with hot water.** Fill three plastic foam cups with hot water. Place one spoon in each cup. Wait 1 minute.
4. Gently touch each spoon. **Record** your **observations**.
5. Touch the three mugs. **Record** your **observations**.
6. Fill each mug with hot water. Carefully touch each handle every 30 seconds for 2 minutes. **Record** what you **observe**.

Temperature of Objects			
	Wooden Spoon	**Plastic Spoon**	**Metal Spoon**
Dry			
After 1 minute			

	Ceramic Mug	**Plastic Mug**	**Metal Mug**
Dry			
After 30 seconds			
After 60 seconds			
After 90 seconds			
After 120 seconds			

Name _____

Investigate Log

Draw Conclusions

1. **Compare** your **observations** of the spoons and the mugs before and after the water was used.

   _____

   _____

   _____

2. **Inquiry Skill—*Draw Conclusions*** Draw a conclusion about the way thermal energy travels through different substances. Write your conclusion down and compare it with a classmate's.

   _____

   _____

   _____

Inquiry Skill Tip

If you have trouble **drawing a conclusion**, try drawing a picture! You can use a drawing or a diagram to summarize the results of an investigation and better understand what happened.

Investigate Self-Assessment	Agree	Not Sure	Disagree
I followed the instructions for observing differences in how fast objects became warm.			
I obeyed safety instructions by wearing goggles and being careful around the hot water.			
I was able to **draw a conclusion** about the way thermal energy travels through different substances.			

Use with pages 556–557.   (page 2 of 3)   Lab Manual   LM 163

Name _____

Date _____

Investigate Log

Independent Inquiry

Repeat the Investigate, using ice-cold water instead of hot water. Before you add the water, predict what will happen in each case.

Materials

Here are some materials that you might use.
List additional materials that you need.

- safety goggles
- wooden spoon
- plastic spoon
- metal spoon
- 3 plastic foam cups
- ice-cold water
- ceramic mug with handle
- plastic mug with handle
- metal mug with handle

1. What do you predict will happen with the metal, plastic, and wooden spoons? What do you predict will happen with the ceramic, plastic, and metal mugs?

   _____

   _____

2. Conduct your investigation. Record your observations on a table like the one in the Investigate.

3. What conclusion can you draw from the investigation?

   _____

   _____

   _____

LM 164   Lab Manual   Use with page 557.

Name _____
Date _____

Investigate Log

Where's the Light?

Materials

- small object
- flashlight
- poster board

Procedure

1. Place a small object on the middle of your desk.

2. Place a flashlight on its side on your desk. Point the flashlight in the direction of the object.

3. Have your partner stand a piece of poster board on the desk. The poster board should be between the flashlight and the object.

4. Turn on the flashlight. **Observe** the object. Does the light shine on it?

5. Have your partner slide the poster board across your desk just until the light shines on the object. **Observe** and **record** the positions of the object, flashlight, and poster board.

Draw the Positions of the Object, the Flashlight, and the Poster Board	Does the light shine on the object?

Use with pages 564–565.   Lab Manual   LM 165

Name _____

Investigate Log

Draw Conclusions

1. What kind of line would you draw to connect the object and the light?

   _____

2. **Inquiry Skill—*Infer*** Scientists **infer**, based on their observations. **Infer** what the path of light is like from the flashlight to the object.

   _____

   _____

Inquiry Skill Tip

Think about how **inferring** is different from guessing. When you guess, you choose an answer at random. Without prior knowledge about the question, your chances of guessing the correct answer aren't good. When you **infer**, you consider the meanings of observations. Observations are clues to help you find the most likely answer.

Investigate Self-Assessment	Agree	Not Sure	Disagree
I followed the directions for this investigation.			
I observed whether the light could shine on the object.			
I **inferred** what the path of the light is like.			

LM 166   Lab Manual   (page 2 of 3)   Use with pages 564–565.

Name _____

Date _____

Investigate Log

Independent Inquiry

Does light always behave the same way? Write a hypothesis. Repeat the activity. Experiment with the angle of the flashlight as it points toward the object. Check your hypothesis.

Materials

Here are some materials that you might use. List additional materials that you need.

- small object
- poster board
- flashlight

1. Write your hypothesis for this investigation.

   _____

   _____

2. Record the positions of the flashlight and your observations in the table below.

Flashlight Position	Observations

3. Did your observations support your hypothesis? Explain.

   _____

Use with page 565.   (page 3 of 3)   Lab Manual   LM 167

Name _____
Date _____

Investigate Log

Making Rainbows

Materials

prism | sheet of white paper | sheet of red paper | sheet of black paper | clear tape

Procedure

1. Cut a narrow slit in the sheet of black paper. Tape the paper to the bottom of a window. Pull down the blinds to make a narrow beam of sunlight.

2. Hold the prism in the beam of light over a sheet of white paper. Slowly turn the prism until it makes a rainbow on the paper.

3. Look closely at the paper. What do you see? **Record** your **observations**.

4. Repeat Steps 2 and 3, using a sheet of red paper.

Position of the Prism	Observations
Over white paper	
Over red paper	

LM 168 Lab Manual   (page 1 of 3)   Use with pages 572–573.

Name _____

Investigate Log

Draw Conclusions

1. How does a prism change sunlight?

   _____

   _____

2. How was the light you saw on the white paper different from the light you saw on the red paper?

   _____

   _____

   _____

Inquiry Skill Tip

When you **predict** what will happen in an investigation, think about the pattern of things that have happened before. Then decide what would happen if that pattern were to continue with just one variable changed.

3. **Inquiry Skill—***Predict* Scientists **predict** what might happen based on patterns or experiences. What do you **predict** you would see if you used the prism to shine sunlight on a piece of blue paper?

   _____

   _____

Investigate Self-Assessment	Agree	Not Sure	Disagree
I followed the directions for making rainbows.			
I held the prism so that sunlight would shine through it.			
I **predicted** what I would see if I used the prism to shine sunlight on a piece of blue paper.			

Use with pages 572–573.   (page 2 of 3)   Lab Manual   LM 169

Name _____
Date _____

Investigate Log

Independent Inquiry

To find out if your prediction is correct, plan and conduct a simple investigation. Remember to use blue paper.

Materials

Here are some materials that you might use.
List additional materials that you need.

- prism
- sheet of blue paper

1. What will your investigation test?

_____

_____

2. Describe what you did and what you observed.

_____

_____

_____

3. Did your observations agree with your prediction? Explain.

_____

_____

_____

LM 170   Lab Manual   (page 3 of 3)   Use with page 573.

Name _____

Date _____

Investigate Log

Make a Maraca

Materials

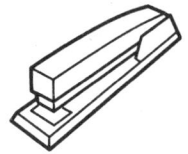

empty paper-towel roll   stapler   masking tape   dried rice   dried beans

Procedure

1. Flatten one end of a paper-towel roll. Fold it over and staple it closed. Put tape over the staples to protect your hands.

2. Put a handful of dried rice and dried beans into the roll.

3. Flatten the open end of the roll. Don't let the rice and beans leak out. Fold over the end of the roll and staple it closed. Tape over the staples. You have made a maraca!

4. Shake the maraca gently a few times. If it leaks beans or rice, check the ends and tape them again. **Observe** the sound it makes.

5. Shake the maraca with more force. **Observe** the sound it makes now.

	Sound Made by the Maraca
Shaken gently	
Shaken harder	

Use with pages 582–583.   (page 1 of 3)   Lab Manual   LM 171

Name _____

Investigate Log

Draw Conclusions

1. How does a maraca make sound?

   _____

   _____

2. **Inquiry Skill—***Compare* Scientists **compare** to learn how things are alike or different. How did the sounds **compare** in Step 4 and Step 5?

   _____

   _____

Inquiry Skill Tip

When you **compare** sounds, it may help to hear the sounds several times each, one after the other. Think about whether the sounds are soft or loud. Is each sound high, like the chirping of a bird? Or is it low, like a foghorn?

Investigate Self-Assessment	Agree	Not Sure	Disagree
I followed the directions for making a maraca.			
I was careful when using the stapler, and I taped over the staples to protect my hands.			
I **compared** the sounds I heard when I shook the maraca gently and when I shook it with more force.			

LM 172   Lab Manual   (page 2 of 3)   Use with pages 582–583.

Name _____

Date _____

Investigate Log

Independent Inquiry

How could you change the maraca's sound? Write a hypothesis. Then plan and conduct a simple investigation to find out.

Materials

Here are some materials that you might use. List additional materials that you need.

- empty paper-towel roll
- stapler
- dried rice
- dried beans
- masking tape

1. Write a hypothesis about how you can change the maraca and the effect you believe it will have on the maraca's sound.

   _____

2. Describe how you changed the maraca and the difference it made in the maraca's sound.

   _____

3. Did your observations agree with your hypothesis? Explain.

   _____

Use with page 583.

Name _____

Date _____

Unit Inquiry Log

Unit F

Make an Obstacle Course

1. **Observe and Ask Questions**

   How are motion, speed, time, and distance related? Design an experiment using a marble and an inclined plane. Make a list of questions you have about motion. Then circle a question you want to investigate.

   _____

2. **Form a Hypothesis**

   Write a hypothesis. A hypothesis is a suggested answer to the question you are testing.

   _____

3. **Plan an Experiment**

   Identify and Control Variables

   To plan your experiment, you must first identify the important variables. Complete the statements below.

   The variable I will change is

   _____.

   The variables I will observe or measure are

   _____.

   The variables I will keep the same, or *control*, are

   _____.

LM 174   Lab Manual   (page 1 of 4)   Use with page 593.

Name _____

Unit Inquiry Log

Develop a Procedure and Gather Materials Write the steps you will follow to set up an experiment and collect data.

_____
_____
_____
_____
_____
_____
_____

Use extra sheets of blank paper if you need to write down more steps.

Materials List Look carefully at all the steps of your procedure, and list all the materials you will use. Be sure that your teacher approves your plan and your materials list before you begin.

_____
_____
_____
_____

Use with page 593.

Name _____

Unit Inquiry Log

4. Conduct the Experiment

Gather and Record Data Follow your plan and collect data. Use the table below or a table you design to record your data. **Observe** carefully. **Record** your observations and be sure to note anything unusual or unexpected.

Obstacle Course Length (cm)	Time (sec)	Speed (cm/sec)

Name _____

Unit Inquiry Log

Interpret Data Make a graph of the data you have collected. Plot the data on a sheet of graph paper or use a software program.

5. **Draw Conclusions and Communicate Results**

   Compare the **hypothesis** with the data and the graphs. Then answer these questions.

   1. Given the results of the experiment, do you think the hypothesis was correct? Explain.

      _____

      _____

   2. How would you revise the hypothesis? Explain.

      _____

      _____

   3. What else did you **observe** during the experiment?

      _____

      _____

Prepare a presentation for your classmates to **communicate** what you have learned. Display your data table and graph.

Investigate Further

Write another hypothesis that you might investigate.

_____

_____

Use with page 593.   Lab Manual LM 177

Name _____
Date _____

Investigate Log

Make It Move

Materials

clay

string (about 25 cm long)

Procedure

1. Mold a piece of clay into a ball. Mold another piece into a ring.

2. Make the ball move in a straight line. Make it move at different speeds. **Record** your **observations**.

3. Make your ball zigzag. **Record** your **observations**.

4. Thread the string through the hole in the ring. Tie the string to the ring. Hold the string by the end. Make the ring swing back and forth and then in a circle. **Record** your **observations**.

5. **Communicate** your **observations** by making drawings of each movement.

Name _____

Investigate Log

Draw Conclusions

1. Record how you made the objects move.

Path of Motion	How the Object Was Pushed or Pulled
straight and fast	
straight and slow	
zigzag	
back and forth	
round and round	

Inquiry Skill Tip

When you **interpret data**, look for patterns. Are there any number patterns? Do any patterns repeat? Can you sort the data into similar groups?

2. Inquiry Skill—*Interpret Data* When you **interpret data**, you explain what the data means. What did you do to make the objects move in different directions?

_____

_____

Investigate Self-Assessment	Agree	Not Sure	Disagree
I molded the clay into a ball and a ring.			
I followed the directions to move the ball and ring in different ways.			
I **interpreted data** in the table to determine how my actions affected the motion of the objects.			

Use with pages 598–599.

Name _____
Date _____

Investigate Log

Independent Inquiry

Plan an experiment with a different object, by itself and on the string. Try to move it each way you moved the ball and the ring.

Materials

Here are some materials that you might use.
List additional materials that you need.

- clay
- string (about 25 cm long)

1. What will your investigation determine?

   _____

   _____

2. Use the table below to summarize the paths of the object and how you made the object move each time.

Path of Motion	How the Object Was Pushed or Pulled

3. What can you conclude about how objects move?

   _____

   _____

LM 180   Lab Manual   Use with page 599.

Name _____

Date _____

Investigate Log

Speed Ramp

Materials

- books
- metric ruler
- cookie sheet
- penny
- block
- rubber eraser

Procedure

1. Use the table below for this investigation.

2. Stack the books about 5 cm high. **Record** how high the pile is.

3. Lay one end of the cookie sheet on the books to make a ramp.

4. Work with a partner. Place the penny, the block, and the eraser at the top of the cookie sheet. Let the objects go at the same time.

5. **Record** how fast each item traveled. Use words such as *fastest*, *slowest*, and *did not move*.

6. Add books to make your stack about 10 cm high. Repeat Steps 3–5.

7. Add books to make the stack about 15 cm high. Repeat Steps 3–5.

Object	Height of Books (cm)	Speed
Penny		
Block		
Eraser		

Use with pages 608–609. Lab Manual LM 181

Name _____

Investigate Log

Draw Conclusions

1. **Compare** the speeds of the sliding objects. **Record** your **observations**.

   _____

   _____

2. **Inquiry Skill—*Infer*** When you **infer**, you make a guess based on what you observe. **Infer** why the speeds of the objects changed.

   _____

   _____

Inquiry Skill Tip

Check that an **inference** fits the data and makes sense. *Ask:* Does my inference agree with the measurements or data? Does it agree with what I know about how the world works?

Investigate Self-Assessment	Agree	Not Sure	Disagree
I made a ramp with books and a cookie sheet.			
I used the ruler to measure the height of the books.			
I **inferred** why the speeds of the objects changed when I changed the starting height.			

LM 182   Lab Manual   (page 2 of 3)   Use with pages 608–609.

Name _____
Date _____

Investigate Log

Independent Inquiry

Predict how your results would change if you coated the cookie sheet with oil. Try it. Record your observations.

Materials

Here are some materials that you might use.
List additional materials that you need.

- metric ruler
- rubber eraser
- books
- block
- cookie sheet
- oil
- penny

1. Predict what will happen if you repeat the investigation with oil on the cookie sheet.

   _____

   _____

2. Conduct the investigation. Use this table to record your observations.

Object	Height of Books (cm)	Speed
Penny		
Block		
Eraser		

3. Summarize and explain your results.

   _____

   _____

   _____

Name _____
Date _____

Investigate Log

Two Kinds of Waves

Materials

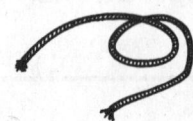

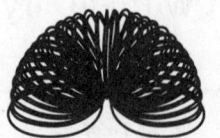

rope about 2 meters long

spring toy

Procedure

1. Hold one end of the rope. Your partner will hold the other end. Let the rope hang loosely between you.

2. Move one end of the rope gently up and down as your partner holds the other end still. Then move the rope faster. **Observe** what happens.

3. Put the coiled spring toy on a table or on the floor. Have your partner hold one end still. Push the other end of the toy about 10 cm toward your partner. Then pull and push that end backward and forward. **Observe** what happens.

4. **Record** your **observations** by making diagrams for Steps 2 and 3.

Diagram of Rope Movement	Diagram of Spring Movement

LM 184   Lab Manual   (page 1 of 3)   Use with pages 618–619.

Name _____

Investigate Log

Draw Conclusions

1. How did the force you used on the rope affect it? What happened when you moved it faster?

   _____

   _____

   _____

2. **Inquiry Skill—*Compare*** When you **compare** things, you look at how they are alike. **Compare** the movements of the waves in the rope with the waves in the toy.

   _____

   _____

   _____

Inquiry Skill Tip

When you **compare** two objects, such as diagrams, pictures, or other representations, lay them side-by-side for comparision. When you **compare** two events, look at tables, charts, or other summaries that show the data or observations of the events.

Investigate Self-Assessment	Agree	Not Sure	Disagree
I followed the directions for moving the rope and the coiled spring toy.			
I drew diagrams to show the motions of both objects.			
I **compared** the movements of the waves in the rope with the waves in the toy.			

Use with pages 618–619.   (page 2 of 3)   Lab Manual   LM 185

Name _____
Date _____

Investigate Log

Independent Inquiry

What do you predict will happen when you move the coiled spring toy in the same way you moved the rope? Try it and see.

Materials

Here are some materials that you might use.
List additional materials that you need.

- coiled spring toy

1. Predict what will happen when you move the coiled spring toy like you moved the rope.

   _____

   _____

2. Conduct the investigation. Draw a diagram in the space below to record your observations.

Diagram of Movement

3. Was your prediction correct? What can you conclude about how to make a wave that moves up and down?

   _____

   _____

   _____

LM 186   Lab Manual   (page 3 of 3)   Use with page 619.

Name _____

Date _____

Investigate Log

Work with Me

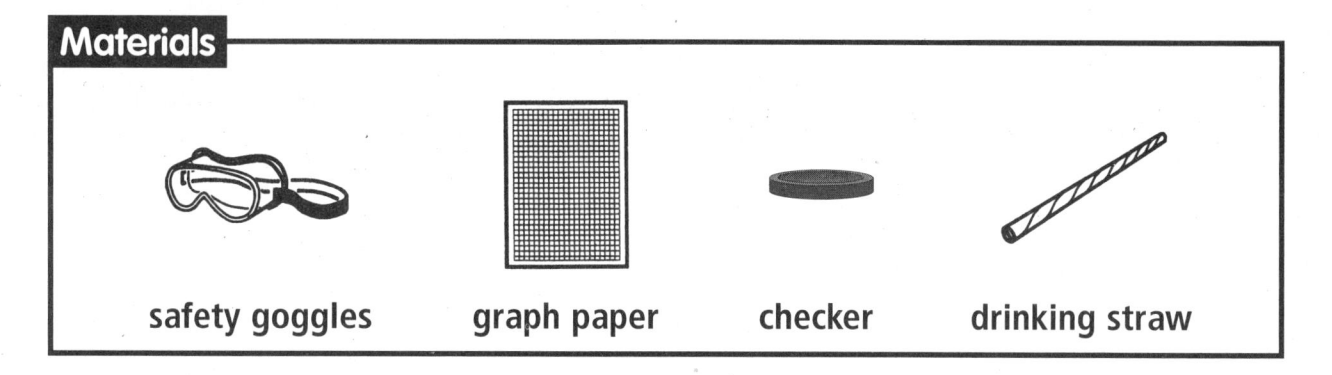

Materials

safety goggles   graph paper   checker   drinking straw

Procedure

1 **CAUTION: Put on the safety goggles.** Work with a partner. On the piece of graph paper, make a start line. Place the checker on the graph paper behind the line.

2 Put one end of the straw in your mouth, and touch the other end to one edge of the checker. Blow hard through the straw.

3 Place the checker back at the same point on the paper. Have your partner press down on the checker while you repeat Step 2. **Record** your observations.

Action	Observation
First time blowing through straw	
Second time blowing through straw	

Use with pages 632–633. (page 1 of 3) Lab Manual **LM 187**

Name _____

Investigate Log

Draw Conclusions

1. Was the force of blowing on the checker the same or different each time? Explain.

   _____
   _____
   _____

> **Inquiry Skill Tip**
>
> You can use many tools to **measure** the size of objects. Any tool that you use should have units that are equal in size.

2. Was the result the same or different each time? Explain.

   _____
   _____

3. **Inquiry Skill—***Measure* Scientists often **measure** things during an experiment. How could you use the graph paper to measure how far the checker moved?

   _____
   _____

Investigate Self-Assessment	Agree	Not Sure	Disagree
I followed the directions for this investigation.			
I wore safety goggles and obeyed safety rules.			
I used the paper to **measure** how much the checker moved.			

LM 188   Lab Manual   (page 2 of 3)   Use with pages 632–633.

Name _____
Date _____

Investigate Log

Independent Inquiry

Predict how using a stack of two checkers might affect your results each time. Try it!

Materials

Here are some materials that you might use.
List additional materials that you need.

- checkers
- graph paper
- drinking straw
- safety goggles

1. Write your prediction.

   _____

2. Predict the distances that the single checker and the stacked checkers will move each time. Measure after each move. Record your data.

Trial	Single Checker Predicted Distance (cm)	Single Checker Actual Distance (cm)	Stacked Checkers Predicted Distance (cm)	Stacked Checkers Actual Distance (cm)
1				
2				

3. Explain how the outcome of this investigation was the same as or different from your prediction.

   _____

   _____

Use with page 633.   (page 3 of 3)   Lab Manual   LM 189

Name _____
Date _____

Investigate Log

Help from Simple Machines

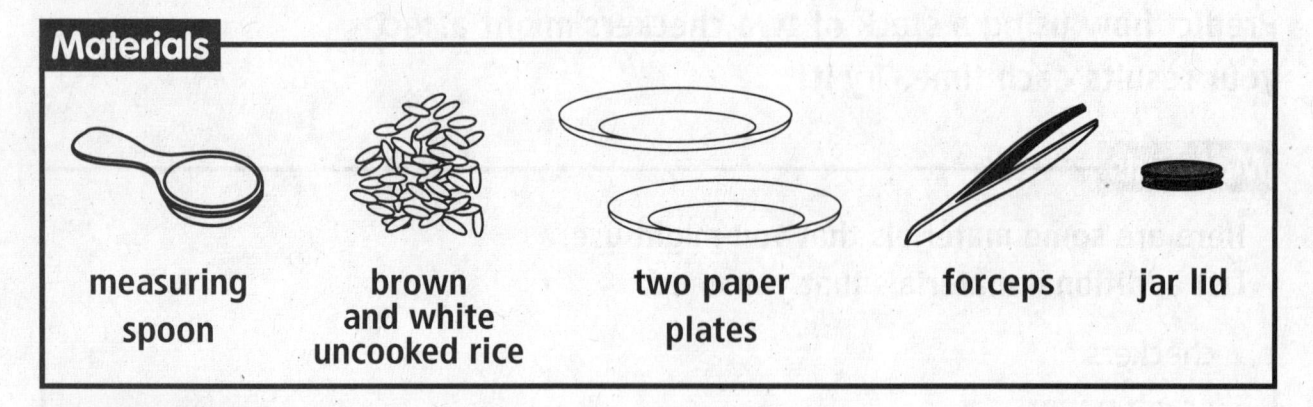

Materials

measuring spoon — brown and white uncooked rice — two paper plates — forceps — jar lid

Procedure

1. Measure out one tablespoon of white rice. Place it in the jar lid. Do the same with the brown rice.
2. Mix the two types of rice inside the lid.
3. Use your fingers to separate the types of rice. **Record** your observations.
4. Put the rice you separated back in the lid. Mix the rice again.
5. This time, use the forceps to separate the types of rice. **Record** your observations.

Method of Separation	Observations
Fingers	
Forceps	

LM 190   Lab Manual   (page 1 of 3)   Use with pages 642–643.

Name _____

Investigate Log

Draw Conclusions

1. Which way of separating the rice grains was easier? Why?

   _____

   _____

2. Which would be a safer way of handling food, using your fingers or using forceps?

   _____

3. **Inquiry Skill—***Predict* Do you think using a spoon to separate the rice would be faster than using forceps? **Predict** which one you think might be faster. Then repeat the Investigate using a spoon and forceps to find out.

   _____

   _____

Inquiry Skill Tip

To **predict** what might happen in an investigation, gather data from other similar investigations. Look at the data for clues about what might happen in your investigation.

Investigate Self-Assessment	Agree	Not Sure	Disagree
I made observations that helped me with this investigation.			
I used the measuring spoon to **measure** out the rice.			
I was able to **measure** the amount of time I took to separate the rice.			

Use with pages 642–643. (page 2 of 3) **Lab Manual** LM 191

Name _____
Date _____

Investigate Log

Independent Inquiry

You have measured how long it took to separate the rice. Compare your time with four other classmates by making a bar graph. Were there differences? Why do you think so?

Materials

Here are some materials that you might use.
List additional materials that you need.

- graph paper

1. Write the sorting time for each of the four classmates.

_____

_____

2. Use the times to make a bar graph like the one shown.

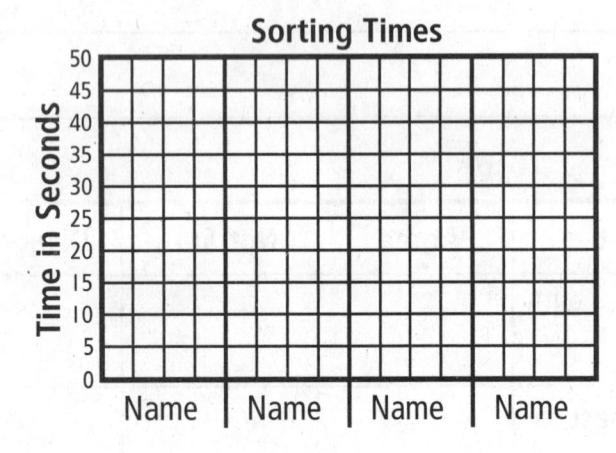

Sorting Times

(Time in Seconds: 0, 5, 10, 15, 20, 25, 30, 35, 40, 45, 50)
(Name | Name | Name | Name)

3. Do the results of your investigation agree with those of your classmates? Explain.

_____

_____

LM 192   Lab Manual   (page 3 of 3)   Use with page 643.

Name _____
Date _____

Investigate Log

Inclined to Help

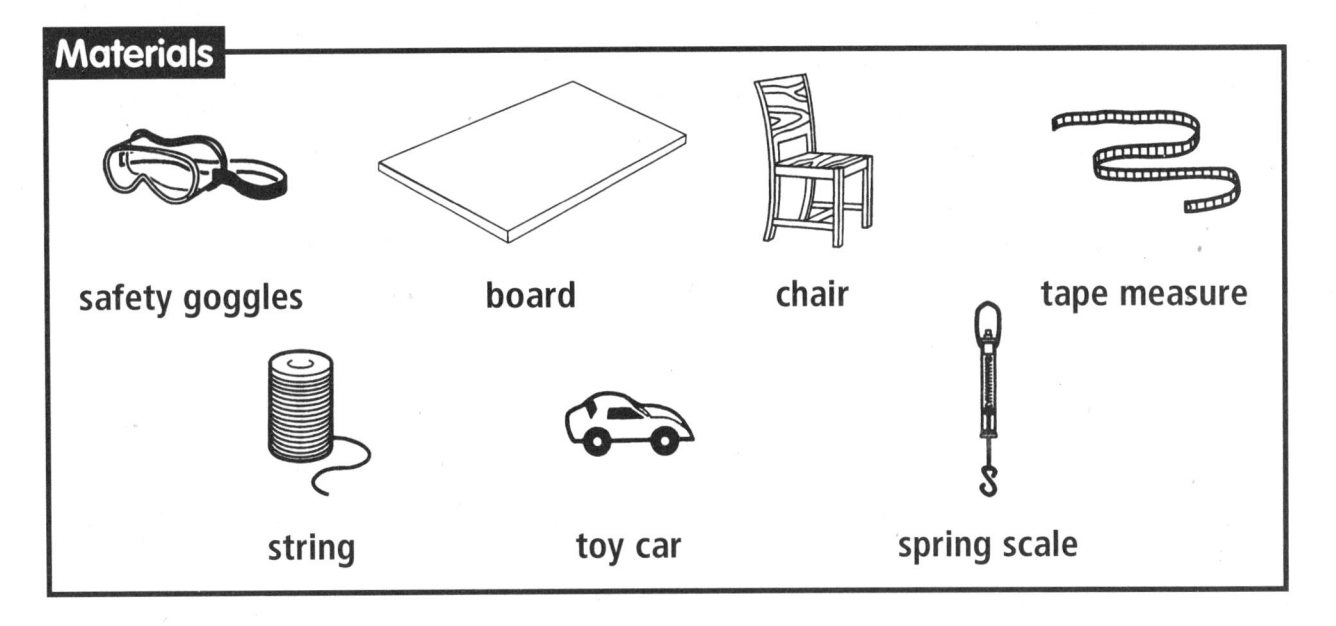

Materials

safety goggles   board   chair   tape measure

string   toy car   spring scale

Procedure

1. **CAUTION:** Put on safety goggles. Use the board to make a ramp from the floor to the chair seat. Use the tape measure to find the distance from the floor to the seat. **Measure** straight up and along the ramp. **Record** both distances.

2. Tie a loop of string to the toy car. Attach the spring scale to the string.

3. Hold on to the spring scale, and lift the car from the floor straight up to the chair seat. **Record** the force shown on the scale.

4. Hold on to the spring scale, and slowly pull the car up the ramp from the floor to the chair seat. **Record** the force shown on the scale.

	Distance (cm)	Times	Force (newtons)	Equals	Work (newton-centimeters)
No ramp		×		=	
Ramp		×		=	

Use with pages 654–655.

Lab Manual   LM 193

Name _____

Investigate Log

Draw Conclusions

1. How did the ramp affect the force needed to lift the car?

   _____

   _____

2. How did the ramp affect the distance?

   _____

3. **Inquiry Skill**—*Interpret Data* Scientists **interpret data** to draw conclusions. What conclusions can you draw from your data?

   _____

   _____

Inquiry Skill Tip

When you **interpret data**, you decide what the data means. Interpreting data involves other processes, such as inferring and drawing conclusions.

Investigate Self-Assessment	Agree	Not Sure	Disagree
I followed the directions for this investigation.			
I used a tape measure and spring scale to make measurements.			
I **interpreted data** to make conclusions about what I observed.			

LM 194 Lab Manual (page 2 of 3) Use with pages 654–655.

Name _____
Date _____

Investigate Log

Independent Inquiry

What might affect the force needed to lift the car?
Plan and conduct a simple investigation to test
some variables.

Materials

Here are some materials that you might use.
List additional materials that you need.

- safety goggles
- board
- chair
- tape measure
- string
- toy car
- spring scale

1. Write a prediction for your investigation.

   _____

   _____

2. Use the following table to record your measurements.

Method of Lifting	Force (newtons)

3. What can you conclude from your results?

   _____

   _____

Use with page 655.   Lab Manual   LM 195

Science Fair Project Ideas

Plants in Space

Design an experiment to determine if plants can grow aboard the space shuttle. Obtain 4 rose tubes from a florist. Place a plant seedling through each of the rubber stoppers, fill the tubes with water, and put the stoppers on the tubes. Then attach one tube to each blade of a tabletop or floor fan. On the slowest setting, allow the plants to grow for about one week. Describe and display your results. You should relate how the plants in the experiment demonstrated the requirements of plants aboard the space shuttle.

Fur, Feathers, and Fat

You will design a test to discover the insulation value of various types of body coverings. Wrap one thermometer in fur, one in feathers, and one in lard. Place all three thermometers in a bowl of ice water. You should record the changes in temperature every 30 seconds for 2 minutes for the three thermometers. You should then analyze and display your results.

Science Fair Project Ideas

My Favorite Prairie

You will design an experiment to demonstrate prairie restoration. Ask an adult for a plot of land in a yard. The plot can be marked off with stakes and string and not mowed for the next few months. Every week you can measure the growth of the plants and record any new plants that invade the plot. Record the differences in grasses and flowering weeds and relate how the plot is similar to a prairie.

Eyes and Ears for Survival

You will analyze the eyes and ears of predators and prey. Divide a display into halves and label one half "Predator" and the other half "Prey." Gather pictures of animals. Decide if an animal is a predator or prey and then place the pictures under the correct heading on the display. You should first describe each animal's vision and placement of its eyes, and then describe each animal's hearing and the placement of its ears. You can use the information on the display board to analyze how predators and prey use their eyes and ears to survive.

Protecting Art Treasures

Construct a model to determine the best way to preserve statues. Obtain three pieces of chalk. Seal one piece of chalk with oil, seal another piece with clear fingernail polish, and leave the last piece unsealed. Place the chalk in vinegar. Observe the chalk over time and then record and display your results.

Science Fair Project Ideas

Expanding Mountains

It's time to make a model of a mountain! Ask yourself questions such as these: What could simulate expansion due to water freezing? What could simulate a sandy surface? What could simulate a surface made of clay? Once the model has been made, place it outside to "weather."

Baked Earth

Place an apple in a pie pan and then ask an adult to place the pie pan in a heated oven. The apple should be baked at 350 degrees for about 30 minutes and then allowed to cool. Discuss how the heating and cooling of the apple is like the heating and cooling of Earth. Illustrate your conclusions with photographs or drawings to show how the cooled apple peel represents landforms on Earth's crust.

Preferred Soil

Do an experiment to find out what type of soil earthworms prefer. Place three different types of soil in a plastic terrarium in three sections. Obtain earthworms and place them on top of the soil in the terrarium. After 24 hours, dig up the earthworms and count how many earthworms were in each type of soil. Make a graph and display your results.

Science Fair Project Ideas

Ice Needs Room

You can design an experiment to demonstrate that equal amounts of water and ice take up different amounts of space. Fill two film canisters with water. Put the lids on them, and then place one film canister in the freezer. One should be left out of the freezer as the control. You can describe and display your results to show how water that freezes in rocks can cause changes to the rocks.

Air Here and There

Design an experiment to determine where air is found. You can fill a bucket with water and place various objects in the water. If bubbles appear on the surface of the objects, water rushed in and air rushed out. Soil, rocks, flower pots, and shells can be tested. Describe and display results and discuss your conclusions.

Window Dressings

You can design an experiment to determine the insulating quality of various window treatments. Seal a shoe box completely with tape and insert a thermometer into a small hole in the lid. One end of the shoe box should be cut out. Then shine a heat lamp at the open end. You can test various products to cover the opening, such as cloth for curtains and wood for shutters. If you test tinted glass, ask an adult to help. Record the temperature and display the results.

LM 199

Science Fair Project Ideas

Air Race

Design an experiment to demonstrate that air has oxygen. You can use three glass jars of different sizes and three candles. Clay can be used to stand the candles on metal lids. Ask an adult to light the candles for you. Time how long each candle burns once the jar is placed over it, and describe your results.

Rust Prevention

Design an experiment to determine the best method to prevent rust. You can use 3 iron nails. One nail can be treated with spray paint and the other nail with cooking oil, leaving one nail without any treatment to be the control. Ask an adult for help. Each nail should be placed in a self-sealing sandwich bag with an equal amount of water added. Measure the amount of rust on each over time and then graph and display your results.

Science Fair Project Ideas

Potential Toys

Design and make a toy that stores energy. Make an origami frog. What happens to the frog when you push on its bottom? On the display board, describe how various forms of energy are stored in toys and then describe how energy is released. Define potential energy and kinetic energy.

Smooth Steps

After you have learned to measure work using spring scales, compare the "work" different sports shoes do as a result of friction. The soles of different sports shoes are purposely designed to either increase or decrease friction. Design and make a ramp to test the friction component of these shoes. You can chart and compare your results. What happens when the shoes are frozen? What happens when they are heated?

Frictionless Fabrics

You can design and conduct an experiment to determine the best fabrics for swimwear worn by racers. Obtain fabric samples of equal size. Drop the fabrics in water. You can then measure which fabric has less drag and drops to the bottom first. Your results should be graphed and displayed.

DISCARDED
MILLSTEIN LIBRARY

MILLSTEIN LIBRARY
UNIVERSITY OF PITTSBURGH
AT GREENSBURG